A SWEET TASTE OF THE LAST SLICE

In memory of those on the other side —

Ruth E. Reitan

A SWEET TASTE OF THE LAST SLICE

REMINDERS, MEMORIES, AND MUSINGS OF A HOSPICE NURSE

RuthiE Neilan
RN, BSN, CHPN, MA (Expressive Arts Therapy)

RuthiE Neilan has written this account based on her memories and documented evidence of these patient experiences and events. Due to the nature of this memoir, the patients described are all deceased, and their real first names are used. Whenever possible, the families of these individuals have verbally permitted the use of their loved one's story for inclusion in this book. The locations and facilities included are actual, however, to maintain the anonymity of those who were not patients, the author has changed some of the names when getting formal permission was not possible.

Copyright © 2024 by RuthiE Neilan

All rights reserved. No part of this book may be reproduced or transmitted in any form or by any means, electronic or mechanical, including photocopying, recording, or any information storage and retrieval system, without permission in writing from the author.

ISBN: 978-1-6653-0858-8 – Paperback
eISBN: 978-1-6653-0859-5 – eBook

These ISBNs are the property of BookLogix for the express purpose of sales and distribution of this title. The content of this book is the property of the copyright holder only. BookLogix does not hold any ownership of the content of this book and is not liable in any way for the materials contained within. The views and opinions expressed in this book are the property of the Author/Copyright holder, and do not necessarily reflect those of BookLogix.

Library of Congress Control Number: 2024908144

Printed in the United States of America   042924

⊗This paper meets the requirements of ANSI/NISO Z39.48-1992 (Permanence of Paper)

This book is dedicated to MSB.

CONTENTS

THE BEGINNING

Foreword	xi
Conversation with a Star	xv
Preface	xvii
Introduction	xix

PART 1　SWEET SOULS

A Beautiful Way to Die	3
First Time Out	21
Norma and Joe	29
Peace with the Smiths	45
Jim: A Window in Time	51
Brian	83

PART 2 THE FLUTE

Finding My Other Voice	93
Rebecca	111
Dee	115
Nancy	125
Beth	139
Leya	147
Gonzales	157

PART 3 SNIPPETS

Steve	173
Church	175
Jane	177
Georgia	181
Catherine's Complaints	185
Faye	189
Not Going to Live Like This	193

PART 4 THE END

And, in Conclusion...	*201*
Acknowledgments	*209*

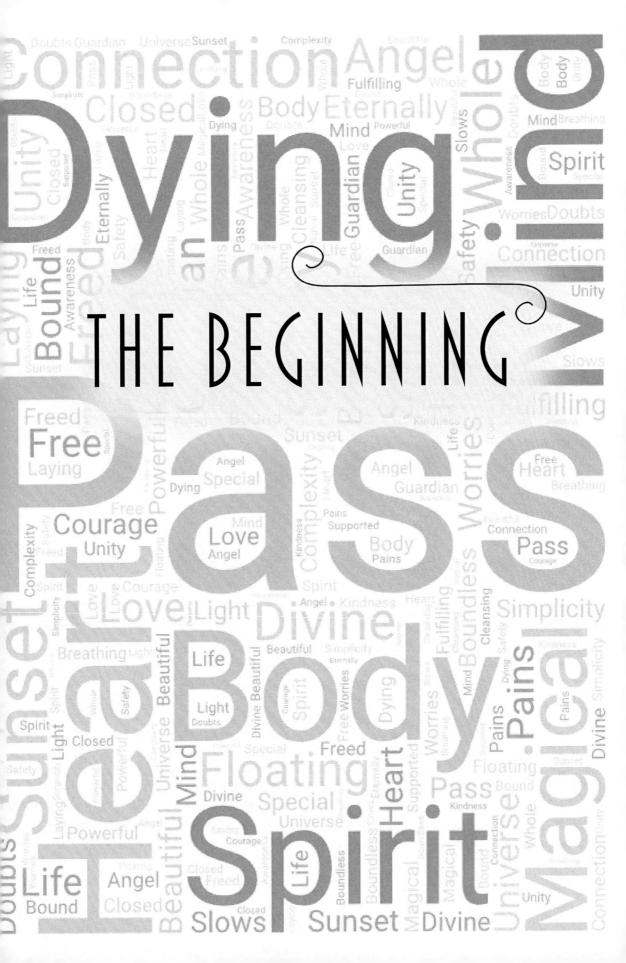

FOREWORD

Collaborating with RuthiE Neilan on this evocative collection of hospice stories has been an experience that I will never forget. Exacting, straightforward, intuitive, and brilliant, she is a woman with a heaping heart. RuthiE has become a spirit to which I aspire. It is remarkable how she has documented her well-lived life with stories, letters, songs, and the grit it takes to understand the beauty of love and the necessity of death without resistance.

RuthiE's musings and memories of her hospice patients over the years are a heartwarming reminder that life never ends when we can bask in the memories of all whom we touch. RuthiE's deathbed stories are brimming with warmth, wisdom, and yes, *life*.

RuthiE Neilan is a *middle* child, which she says may explain her behavior. Her siblings accused her of being the *favorite* child, which may also explain her behavior. RuthiE is a dichotomy, one part fighter and another part fierce protector of the last slices of life.

It might have taken being raised on a small self-sustaining farm that allowed RuthiE to see death as a part of the life cycle. Although clear about life and death, her clarity is not without deep sentimentality.

While the Vietnam war was raging, RuthiE met her beloved husband, Bob, who dropped out of school and enlisted in the Army as a private in September of 1966, eager to join the battle. The night before he was to leave for basic training, he asked RuthiE to marry him.

The two became engaged in 1966. They were married on January 6, 1968. Bob's impressive military career took them all over the world. And, in all of those places, RuthiE managed to stand by her husband, adapt to her new surroundings, and infuse her great love for people into every community. Still, after 55 years of marriage, she is Bob's devoted caretaker, even after his diagnosis of Parkinson's disease and dementia. RuthiE still blushes when she speaks of her husband's earned nickname, MSB (My sweet Bob).

Always walking with her strong spirituality, RuthiE has gracefully and adamantly guided patients to make the ultimate transition with grace. Along the journey, she discovered her other voice, her musical voice. With the help of the Native American flute community and other art therapies, her level of hospice care took on a deeper otherworldly dimension. RuthiE's passion and artistic skills are infectious. Her whole life is a testimony to how art changes lives and makes a peaceful death possible. Additionally, her calm, no-nonsense manner has served her well in honoring the wishes of a patient's last days.

The souls in these stories face death, fearlessly because of their unexpected blessing, RuthiE Neilan. The stories that RuthiE shares are meant to awaken you. *A Sweet Taste of the Last Slice* reminds us how important it is to live life to the fullest until the time comes to lay our burdens down.

Kim Green

CONVERSATION WITH A STAR

I spoke with Venus,

Evening star that shines alone at sunset

Blends with other stars throughout the dark night

Reappears to stand alone.

Before dawn.

Venus informed me.

Laughing and crying spring from the same well

Emotion rises unbidden, without control.

When you awake from a dream

You must write down to capture.

Or it is forgotten.

Venus assures me the dead live on

In my imagination

Laughing, crying, and conversing with

A star.

RuthiE Neilan

PREFACE

"I must do all the good I can for all the people I can; I will never pass this way again." This message came to me "loud and clear" when asked to define my "philosophy of life" as a first-year student in St. Patrick School of Nursing. I was 17 years old. I retired from nursing in 2012 in celebration of my 70th birthday. I continued as a Native flute player until 2021 when Lynette, the co-owner of Casa de la Luz, died unexpectedly, and the business was sold. That same year, my husband was diagnosed with Parkinson's disease, and the next year, we moved to Ohio to live out the last sweet slice of our lives near our daughter and her family. When I turned 80, I realized I need to "finish or forget" this memoir.

I believe I have done all the good I can for all the people I can during my life. Especially my long and loving relationship with MSB, for whom I pledged, as my biblical namesake, Ruth, *pledged, "Wherever you go I will go, and wherever you live I will live. Your people will be my people and your God will be my God"* (New Catholic Bible, St. Joseph edition, Ruth. 1.16).

As the writing of this book came to a close, I wondered, why was it written? And how would it end? I thought about what I have learned and what I have taught. This ancient Celtic blessing for discernment surfaced. It has been a touchstone.

Find the place in you that is between the sun and the moon

Between darkness and dawn

Between the lightning flash and thunder

The question and the answer come together there.

Ancient Celtic poem

INTRODUCTION

"Who among you believes cancer is a beautiful way to die?"

Without a preamble, the petite woman walked confidently to the podium and spoke without a microphone. The crowd responded with a collective gasp. I felt my arm rise slowly. Our speaker nodded, her European accent clipped each word, "*Vell,* I am glad to see at least *three* of you agree with me! *Vee* all will die. Some of us *vill* die suddenly, leaving unfinished business. Some of us *vill* die of cancer. A diagnosis of terminal cancel is a "*vake* up" call on how to live, and THAT'S why cancer is a beautiful way to die."

Dr. Elisabeth Kubler-Ross, a psychiatrist from Switzerland, had recently published *On Death and Dying* and was on a speaking tour. It was 1971. Bob and I were newlyweds; he was a 1st lieutenant assigned to Ft. Carlson, Colorado. I remember it as clearly as it was yesterday.

I was familiar with Dr. Kubler-Ross' work, required reading in the nursing program at USF, and I was delighted to meet her. I was enchanted by her passionate personality. Dr. Kubler-Ross explained she was interested in the "near death" experiences of those who died. However, her supervisors, concerned that the discussion of dying might cause a fatal heart attack, suggested she interview cancer patients because "they are dying anyway." This is the population she worked with and said, "The dying have a lot to teach us."

Dr. Kubler-Ross defines the stages of dying in *On Death and Dying*: denial, anger, bargaining, depression, and acceptance. She described the concepts in detail which were new at the time. She traced the history of hospice care and its philosophy, which was founded in the UK by Dame Cicely Saunders in the late 1960s. Hospice came to the United States as a volunteer grassroots program several years later.

My father was diagnosed with terminal cancer in 1980. It was an excruciatingly painful time for me. I was devastated to discover that there was no hospice in the rural community where he lived. Ten years later, motivated by my desire that no family would suffer, as I had through the challenging time of losing my father, I signed up for hospice volunteer training.

I began writing hospice stories as a volunteer in the 1990s, continued writing after I became certified in hospice nursing in the 2000s, and included more stories from my MA Thesis for Expressive Arts Therapy (2005). I realized through these writings, Dr. Kubler Ross' influence was "ground zero" for my life's work–over 30 years in hospice.

In defending my thesis, *Living with Dying Expressively-Sharing Breath Through Native America Flute,* the examining professor interrupted my opening remarks, "RuthiE, we do not facilitate dying."

I replied, "Well, I do."

The professor nodded approvingly and said, "Carry on."

I asked the class, mostly Europeans unfamiliar with the concept of hospice, to "imagine being the guest of honor at a banquet held on Holy Ground. The world's finest chocolate is served to you for dessert. You are given *a sweet taste of the last slice*. It's like that in hospice," I concluded.

They smiled and nodded. They got it.

PART 1

SWEET SOULS

A BEAUTIFUL WAY TO DIE

"It's time for you to come home." Dad's voice was clear, calm, and unmistakable. The call I expected for months caught me off guard.

I stammered, "Okay, Daddy. I will be there as soon as I can."

I booked a flight "Space-A" (space available) out of Hickam Air Base in Honolulu to Spokane, Washington. The year before, my daughter, Anne Katherine, and I had flown Space-A on a tanker, to be with Mom when she had gall bladder surgery. Mom died of post-op complications two weeks after we returned to Hawai'i, just in time for Anne Katherine to start all-day kindergarten. We were the only passengers on that flight and spent most of the time laying on our bellies, watching through a window in the floor as the tanker refueled planes in the air.

This time we flew on an ordinary passenger plane with seats on both sides of the center aisle. The plane was full. A shopping spree to Hawai'i had been arranged for spouses of soldiers stationed in Alaska. They were told Anne Katherine and I were flying to Spokane because my father was dying. It was a subdued flight to the mainland. I felt sad. It had been less than a year since Mom died, and now, I was anticipating Dad's death.

It is over a three-hour drive from Spokane to the farm where Dad lived and I grew up. We arrived in the midafternoon. Dad was sitting on a bench attached to the wood picnic table in the front yard. The sunlight was dappled with shade from large cottonwood trees that surrounded the yard space. The smell of freshly mowed grass was pungent in the warm air. Dad was the picture of health, I thought. He was wearing his usual bib overalls with a blue shirt, sleeves rolled up past his elbows. Anne Katherine greeted him with a hug, then ran to the tire swing hanging from a rope on the cottonwood next to the front gate. She flopped on her belly, pushed with her feet, and swung up into the air, just as I had done when I was her age. It was good to be home.

I was introduced to Marla, a smiling, young, granola-type woman my sister, Francie, had hired to look after Dad. She was responsible for seeing that Dad was eating, taking vitamins, and getting a good night's sleep. Her high energy felt intrusive, crowding into my space. I thanked Marla for being there, but her help was no longer needed since I was now home. I would look after Dad's needs. She nodded and said, "Glad I was able to be of help." Marla smiled, said goodbye, and left.

Dad and I both expected my visit to be of the "hello and goodbye" variety, lasting no more than a week. My one-week plan quickly morphed into four as I witnessed his rapid decline.

I was caught off guard with feelings of grief. While accepting and anticipating Dad's dying, I realized I had not grieved Mom's death. She was alive the last time I saw her. It was like she hadn't died in my mind. I walked around the house expecting to see her. The emptiness of the house literally felt cold; her absence was a dark void in my heart.

It hit me hard. I cried at the drop of a hat.

A cousin asked, "Why are you crying?"

I tried to explain, touching my hand to my heart, "She's been dead for almost a year! I didn't really KNOW she was dead, until I got home, and she isn't here!"

Francie and I had conspired to get Dad out of Montana as autumn slid into winter. Bob and I had set up a writing space for him on the lanai, where he smoked, drank coffee, and wrote. I do not recall talking about Mom once during the visit.

Thinking back on that time, Dad's visiting us in Hawaii after Mom's death in early September, 1979, was surreal. Mom was the hub of our family. She kept the fire hot, meals cooked, and looked after Dad who spent much of his time sitting at the kitchen table, drinking coffee, smoking "roll your own" Bull Durham, and writing. He wrote letters, essays, and gave advice to politicians. Thoughts and ideas. Every day, pretty much all day.

Dad had been an easy, gracious house guest. He was content except for a "catch" in his upper back. Aspirin "took the edge off." He felt his chiropractor back home could straighten it out. After Francie said that it was still too cold in Montana without a fire, I made an appointment with a local chiropractor.

Dad kept the appointment, reporting, "It didn't help much. The chiropractor wanted X-rays. I said 'no.'"

I asked Dr. Steve, D.O. (doctor of Osteopathy) who lived next door to examine him because of his ongoing pain. Dr. Steve gently palpated dad's spine. His long fingers moved three or four inches down the spine and pointed to an indentation squarely between dad's shoulder blades.

Dr. Steve asked him, "Does this hurt?"

Dad said, "Not any more than anywhere else."

Dr. Steve raised his eyebrows, surprised by the response, he silently gestured for me to place my fingertips where his had been.

I felt the hollow space. "What is this?" I asked.

Dr. Steve replied, "It feels like a separation of the rib from the spine."

I turned to my father and said, "Dad, are you sure this doesn't hurt?"

"Not so I can tell," he replied.

Dad retreated to his lanai alcove and came out to speak to me a short time later. He said he wanted to go home to see his own chiropractor. "I think it is warm enough."

I took him to the airport.

He called a few days later, as promised. "I saw my chiropractor. The X-rays show tumors. I've got cancer. It's inoperable, and I'm not going to take chemo poison. The doctor says I've got a few months."

The news landed like a thud in my heart. "Do you want me to come home?"

"No, I will tell you when it's time," he said.

He had kept his word, and when it was time, I went home.

Remembering Dr. Kubler-Ross' statement, *cancer is a beautiful way to die*, I suggested we bring in hospice. Dad agreed, only to find out there was no hospice. I shouted in my distress, "WHAT DO YOU MEAN THERE IS NO HOSPICE HERE?"

The American Cancer Society loaned a hospital bed that we set up in the living room, close enough to the wall for the telephone cord to reach. There was no hospice team. No nurse, no social worker, no chaplain, no home health aide. We could have used their support.

One night, shortly after we arrived, I was awakened by Dad's shouts, "Ruth! Ruth!"

I grabbed my robe for warmth and dashed into his bedroom. "Daddy, what's wrong?" The linoleum floor was cold on my bare feet. I climbed onto the double bed next to him.

He was sitting straight up. There was just enough light to see his expression of pure delight. "I've figured it out! It's all about forgiveness!"

"Dad, what are you talking about?"

He said, "Life! All that stuff about 'love one another and the Golden Rule.' It's all about forgiveness. You can't have love without forgiving." His expression was calm and radiant. His clear, bright blue eyes matched his pajamas. Dad's voice softened. "If I have ever said or done anything to hurt you, please forgive me."

"No, I can't think of anything. If I have ever said or done anything to hurt you, Dad, please forgive me."

He reached his arms out and wrapped them around me. "You could never hurt me." It was as I remembered him comforting me as a child. I thought I was going to start crying.

A couple of days later when he asked me a medical-related question, I realized I was too emotionally close to the situation.

I said, "There's just one thing, Dad. I can't be a detached professional nurse. I came home as your little girl."

"I understand," he said.

I think he was the only one who really understood. My sisters and I were not close growing up. We reverted to old patterns of behavior and communication—or lack thereof. I also felt very angry knowing there was no hospice. Not to have it available was devastating. I felt isolated, abandoned, and overwhelmed by the questions and expectations. "Because you're the nurse," my sisters and cousins defended their contempt.

Pain was an issue. Dad was either "knocked out cold" or in agony. I remember a telephone conversation with Dr. Baldwin who took over Dr. Murray's practice when he retired. The prescribed dosage of morphine was no longer controlling his pain. Dad needed to take more of it, more often.

I asked, "But won't he become addicted?"

The doctor's voice was kind and patient. After a short pause, he said, "No, he won't become addicted."

I looked back on this question with understanding years later, when families voiced concern about addiction. The reality is twofold; the patient won't live long enough, and morphine is taken to relieve pain, not to get high.

One day, remembering Dr. Kubler-Ross' end-of-life teachings, I asked Dad if he had left anything unsaid or undone.

He asked me to place a call to a lifelong friend and distant cousin in Wyoming. They had been together in Wyoming during the Depression. His family stayed in Wyoming, and my father's family moved to Montana. The two men chatted for over a half hour catching up on the years since they had been together. After they said goodbye, Dad handed me the phone. "Thank you," he said.

I don't remember much of the day-to-day activity of Dad's care except the day I almost set the house on fire. I was standing in the doorway between the kitchen and living room. Dad was on the hospital bed with his head elevated. Anne Katherine was trying to get my attention. She said, "Mom! Mom!" She was tugging on my leg. Then, she wailed loudly, "MOMM-LOOK!" pointing to the right.

The frying pan on the electric stove was on fire! Flames shooting over a foot high, licking the bottom of the cabinets above the stove. I grabbed the handle of the pan with a potholder. In one swift move, I flipped the pan upside down into the empty sink to the right of the stove. The flames were immediately smothered. Disaster averted. I knelt to Anne Katherine's eye level with a hug, apologizing and thanking her for telling me.

It was hot upstairs where Anne Katherine and I slept on a large pallet. A narrow-width 36-inch square floor fan blowing directly on us cooled the air. I would gulp down a shot of Bourbon as a sedative before laying down, utterly exhausted, next to Anne Katherine who would already be asleep.

One night, I was awakened by voices coming from back-lit shadows on the stairs. The memory of the shadows is clear, who made the shadows is not. I heard, "We are taking him to the emergency room. He can't urinate."

Overhearing their mumbled conversation, I muttered, "Okay, fine," then turned over and went back to sleep.

They returned later that evening to say Dad had a catheter

inserted. He was also given a shot for pain which knocked him out.

My sister, Helen, who is an excellent LPN (licensed practical nurse) recently told me, "I took Dad to the ER that night." She had come from out of town to spend the night with him. Helen said, "He wanted somebody with him. When he would call out 'Helen,' I would say, 'I'm here, Dad, what do you need? He would say "Nothing." He just wanted to make sure I was awake with him."

Helen told me, "The night of the trip to the ER, I arrived about 9 o'clock to spend the night. Dad said he hadn't been able to pee all day. I wondered why he waited until I came to tell anyone."

Thinking about this now, I suspect Dad waited for Helen because he knew she was coming. It is possible he remembered my statement, "I can't be your nurse," and she could.

Dad was losing sensation and feeling in his legs. He was quite fascinated with the physical phenomena of dying and asked, "Is this part of the process?"

I guessed that it was and said, "Yes."

We took turns running the bristles of a hairbrush over his lower legs.

"It feels good," Dad had said.

My past orthopedic experiences came into play the day Dad wanted to use the toilet. He was no longer able to stand. My sisters and I lifted him out of bed and placed him on a dining room chair. Then, tilting the chair onto the back legs, scooted dad and chair backwards down the hall on the linoleum floor, into the bathroom. Dad was light enough that two of us lifted him up and sat him on the toilet.

One day that stands out clearly is the day our retired family physician, Dr. Murray, came to visit with a 6-pack of beer. Albeit physician and farmer, they were lifelong friends. Dr. Murray was a young man barely out of medical school with a new practice in our community when Pearl Harbor was attacked. He was drafted into the Army. Dad, a farmer, was exempt.

It galled Dr. Murray that he had missed out on so much while he was away in the Army. To be admitted to St. Patrick's Diploma School of Nursing, a complete physical exam was required with a signature from the doctor. Of course, my parents sent me to Dr. Murray. At the conclusion of the exam, he asked, "I delivered you, didn't I?"

I said, "No, you were away at war."

Dr. Murray said, "Well, hell, I would have delivered you if I had been here!" He signed the paper with a flourish. He and Dad laughed, remembering that October, in 1942, the year of my birth.

I spent most of Dr. Murray's hour-long visit outside so he and Dad could reminisce in private about their long friendship.

As he got into his car, Dr. Murray asked me, "Where are you living now?"

Nonchalantly, I said, "Hawai'i."

He looked at me hard with disbelief. "Well, don't that just beat all to hell! A little girl from Montana living in Hawai'i!" He closed the car door and drove away.

My cousin, Doug, on leave from work in Oregon due to an injury, came to see Dad, too. He confided later, "I came out to the farm to visit Uncle Brainerd because I knew I couldn't come back for his funeral." My cousin, Jim, also came to visit. We had been in the same class in school until he moved with his family to eastern Montana, during our freshman year in high school. We were the "class of 1960." Ironically, it was time for our 20th high school reunion. I had not planned to attend. I was home because Dad was dying. I only had a long mumu in my suitcase, "just in case."

I am glad Jim convinced me to go to the reunion. A few stiff drinks, a good dinner, dancing, a lot of laughs, and breakfast at the 4 B's Café on the way home at midnight were a welcome, rejuvenating break for me.

Another day, Sharleen, my St. Pats nursing school roommate, drove over from Hot Springs and said, "Let's go for a drive. It will give you a break." We call that "respite" today. We drove the back country roads for almost two hours.

When we got back to the house rested and refreshed, my sister, Francie said, "Dad wants to go to the hospital. He says it's time."

By now, Dad was confined to the hospital bed set up in the living room. Francie called for the ambulance and instructed, "No lights, no sirens."

Anne Katherine and I crawled into the back of the ambulance and sat on the floor next to Dad. He was on a stretcher with an oxygen mask covering his nose and mouth. The road was covered with loose gravel between the farm and the paved highway into town. The ambulance was probably going 25 or 30 mph, fast enough for road dust to boil up and pour inside. Anne Katherine leaned forward between the driver and passenger front seats and said sternly, "Slow down! There's a sick man back here!"

Dad smiled.

After we got Dad settled into his new digs at the hospital, he held court; he was well-known and respected. There was a steady stream of visitors. Now that he was in the hospital, it was easier for folks to stop by instead of driving four miles to the farm. St. Luke's is in a community where everyone knows everyone else. Even Rosemary, the Director of Nurses, was a close friend and neighbor.

Anne Katherine was not allowed inside to visit her grandfather. She could only peer through a window and wave to him. I could not believe Rosemary refused to bend the rules, if not for Anne Katherine, for my father, her longtime friend.

One visitor was especially welcome. John had been a foster child in my parents' care. He showed up with a lovely young woman who he introduced as his wife. She was carrying a large bouquet of red flowers. They had made a special effort to dress for the visit to see Dad. John was wearing pressed black trousers and a crisp white shirt. His coal black hair combed; his shoes polished. His petite wife wore a modest dress. John introduced my father to his wife saying, "This is the man who changed my life. He made a difference." To Dad he said, "I want to thank you for everything you taught me."

Dad was especially pleased with the flowers. He said, "I can see them!" I had been unaware of Dad's cloudy vision until then; another sign of life failing.

Dad was not an agnostic, neither was he a churchgoer. He had an open mind and great faith in God, our Creator. One of his favorite Bible verses was Psalm 121 which he recited for me one afternoon. "I lift up my eyes to the hills from whence cometh my help."

Dad's sister, my Aunt Lorena, had recently joined the Mormon church, also called Latter Day Saints (LDS). She wished to have elders from the church bless Dad. I remember three men in dark suits standing beside Dad's bed. I was there with my sisters and Aunt.

After the Mormon elders' blessing, Dad agreed to my request to bring in a priest. He also agreed to Francie inviting her pastor from Pentecostal Life Christian Church. Neither Francie nor I were there when they visited. Both men reported, "all is well with his soul."

It wasn't long before pain became an issue again. Dad was in agony or knocked out cold from an injection of Demerol. I caught up with Dad's attending physician in the hall and said, "I've met Dr. Kubler-Ross; she talked about a 'Brompton's

Cocktail' for pain. It can be self-administered," I said confidently.

Brompton's Cocktail is a liquid mixture served in a small medicine cup. Dad could take sips as needed. It was developed in London, adapted for legal use in the United States by omitting the ingredients heroin and cocaine. It is a mixture of morphine, water, cherry syrup, alcohol, and one of three anti-emetics: Thorazine, Phenergan, or Compazine. (Anti-emetic is a class of drug used to prevent nausea.)

Doctor Baldwin said, "Yes, I am familiar with it. We don't use it unless it is asked for."

"Well, I am asking for it." He nodded, turned, and walked away without comment.

Brompton's Cocktail was extremely effective in controlling Dad's pain. He was comfortable and coherent.

One day Dad waved to Anne Katherine whose face was pressed against the window. He said to me, "You need to get that little girl home."

I nodded absentmindedly, still annoyed at Rosemary for not bending the "no children" rule. Despite my annoyance at her, she even said, "I see you around here so much you might as well reactivate your Montana nursing license and come to work for me. I have a lot of paperwork to catch up on, and there are always phone calls to make."

Another day, Rosemary pulled me aside and said, "What will we do with Francie?" The doctor had wanted to take X-rays of Dad's back, and Francie intervened, saying, "No, he is dying. Why take X-rays?"

"What would be the point?" I said to Rosemary.

A few days later, when I was alone with Dad, he said, "It's time for you to go home."

I asked, "Are you sure?"

He said, "Yes."

My cousin Jack, who has always been more like a brother, agreed to take us to the airport in Missoula, an hour away. I had decided to fly to California to visit Bob's parents on the way to Hawai'i.

I called Francie from San Francisco, and she said, "Dad kept asking, 'Is Ruth on the plane yet?' When Jack finally returned with the report that you were on the plane, Dad closed his eyes and went to sleep."

When I called the next morning, Dad was in a coma. Francie said, "The doctor said it could be hours or days."

I felt torn. Should I go back? Or should I go on? My father had told me when it was time to come and told me when it was time to go. I decided to go on.

It is over a five-hour flight from San Francisco to Honolulu. I stepped off the plane into Bob's waiting arms. He spoke softly into my ear, "He's gone. He died while you were over the ocean." I lifted my face to the sun letting tears mingle with raindrops–a Hawaiian weather phenomenon in which light rain falls while the sun shines. It is called "pineapple juice" and considered a blessing from Heaven. I smiled and cried at my last memory of Dad sitting with the head of his bed elevated. He lifted his right arm at the elbow. Fingers of his right hand curled, cocking his right index finger forward, giving it a little shake in what is known as a "farmer's salute." His last words to me were, "I'll see you later."

Anne Katherine looked up at me and asked, "Mom, why are you laughing and crying?"

I said, "Because Grandpa is in Heaven, sending us blessings."

FIRST TIME OUT

"Take the tomato!" I heard my father's words as I hung up the phone with Judy. She had given me my first hospice volunteer assignment. The dramatic opening music from *Mission Impossible* came to mind. Hanging up with Judy, I had accepted the mission. Just like on *Mission Impossible*, the fuse had been lit.

I had completed volunteer training. Judy Green, Coordinator of Volunteers, called to ask if I would accept the assignment to drive across town, pick up a patient named Mary, and transport her to a skilled nursing facility (SNF) where she had decided to live out the last slice of her life. There was a short time span—she had to be admitted by midafternoon, and it was already approaching one o'clock.

As I rushed to leave, grabbing car keys and purse, I distinctly heard my father's voice saying, "Take the tomato." The command turned my attention to the ripe tomato the size of a small orange I harvested that morning from a planter in the backyard. It was a bright red jewel on the white tiled counter.

"Take the tomato!" my father insisted.

I tried to reason with him, "Why on Earth would I take a tomato?"

As I reached the doorway out to the garage, he spoke again. "Take-the-Tomato!"

"OK! OK!" I relented, scooped up the tomato, tossed it onto the passenger seat of the car, and dashed across town to the address I had been given.

Traffic was light. I pulled into the cul-de-sac in front of the house, ahead of schedule. The door to the house was open. As I got out of the car, a large man, with uncombed hair, wearing a soiled white tee shirt with rumpled slacks was standing on the sidewalk facing the front of my car.

Before I could say, "Hi, I'm RuthiE from hospice-"

He shouted, "Do you THINK you're going to take Mary to the

nursing home in your CAR? I asked for a VAN! I SPECIFICALLY asked for a van. Your car is NOT a van!!" He paced back and forth on the sidewalk, fists clenched, his face red, as I timidly picked up the tomato I had been told to bring and held it in my outstretched hand.

"Look," I said. "I brought you a tomato."

"HA!" he shouted, "You call THAT a tomato?" He turned toward the open door and called in disdain, "Mary, she brought ME a tomato!"

"Oh, how nice," a woman's soft voice floated back. "Why don't you show her your tomatoes dear?"

The big man hesitated and shrugged. Still angry he said, "Oh, alright, come on!" He opened the six-foot gate in the wood fence behind him and beckoned me to follow.

My mouth fell open as I entered an incredible secret space filled with tomato plants. There were cherry tomatoes, grape tomatoes, Roma tomatoes, red, orange, yellow, and green tomatoes, various size plants, bushes, shrubs in pots and in the ground, and unbelievably, a tomato tree. I had never seen anything like it.

As I followed the man on a narrow dirt path that meandered through the quarter-acre garden, I listened to him describe the plants. His tone and face softened. His name was Roger, and he shared his concerns for Mary, his companion of over 30 years, whom he never married. He said he could no longer care for her at home. He wanted her delivered safely to the nursing home. He was concerned Mary would not be able to transfer from her wheelchair into my car. He determined a van would be easier for her to manage.

We entered the house. Roger made tomato sandwiches of thick slices on white bread slathered with mayonnaise while I called the Volunteer Coordinator to discuss the dilemma.

Jan, the Nursing supervisor, would come in her van, and bring Judy. They arrived a short time later. The three of us managed to take Mary from her bed, place her in a wheelchair, and maneuver her into Jan's van. They left immediately to make the admission deadline which they barely made. Roger followed in his car, and I followed in mine. Jan and Judy were waiting for me when I arrived at the SNF (Skilled Nursing Facility) which was to be Mary's new home.

Judy was concerned Mary would be left sitting in the wheelchair in the lobby after she and Jan left. She turned to me and spoke in a whisper, "Can you stay with Mary until she is installed in her bed and comfortable?"

I agreed.

I looked around for Roger. Mary volunteered, "He saw me arrive and get inside. He will come back later to visit." Once the paperwork was completed, the social worker left. I accompanied Mary to her room, trailing behind her wheelchair and two young female care aides. One pushed the wheelchair, the other walked alongside holding Mary's hand, smiling, chatting reassuringly. "You're going to be fine here."

The care aides asked me to wait in the hallway while they changed Mary into a nightgown and put her to bed.

How different this space was from her bed positioned in the living room of her home with Roger. She had left behind a warm, welcoming, loving, and comfortable space. Cream-colored walls, a large poster of the Sacred Heart on the wall behind her head. The statue of Our Lady of Fatima stood with outstretched arms on her bedside table. Large picture windows let in sunshine and a view of the front yard and street beyond. There was nothing like that here. The 8x10-foot room had bright white walls, one framed still life print of a bowl of fruit on the wall facing the foot of the bed, and no window. The head of the bed was elevated enough that Mary and I were at eye level. We made small talk, comparing the starkness of this room to the one she left behind. I felt comfortable in her presence and told her I wished I could stay longer. "My daughter is a student at Bellarmine Prep. The Philomathea Mother's Club meets for Mass today, and I need to leave."

Mary looked at me with sadness in her eyes, then up at the ceiling, and spoke softly, her voice wistful, "Oh it has been so long since I have been to Mass. I wish I could go with you."

Without hesitating, or giving it thought, I said, "Would you like me to bring you Communion?"

When I arrived at Bellarmine Chapel, Father was already vesting in the sacristy. I approached quietly and excused myself with the explanation that I was a hospice volunteer and had just come from a visit.

Father did not look up when he asked, "Would you like to take her Communion?"

I did, each week for almost two months, until I was stopped at the front desk and told, "You can visit Mary, but do not give her Communion!"

"Why not?"

"Because she might choke on it."

I slipped into Mary's room. She was resting, eyes closed, her bed in an upright position. I spoke softly, not to startle her.

"Mary, they told me not to give you Communion because you might choke on it. I wish I had been brave enough to tell the nurse, where to go …"

Mary smiled at me for a moment. I thought I heard her giggle. She said she wanted to receive the Eucharist anyway. I gave her a sip of water, broke off a small piece of the host, put it on her tongue, and followed it with another sip of water.

We shared silent prayer as we did every week. Then Mary turned her face to me and said, "You don't need to come anymore."

"Are you sure?"

"Yes, I am sure."

Judy called the next morning to tell me that Mary died during the night.

A week later I walked down a graveled cemetery road to the graveside service for Mary. I heard someone call my name. Roger lumbered toward me. I had not seen him since the day Mary was admitted to the nursing facility. His hair was slicked down with water. He wore a rumpled brown suit with a clean white shirt and a tie with a food stain on it. His voice was tremulous as the once-angry man gave me a big bear hug.

"Thank you for giving her what I couldn't. It meant a lot to both of us." Roger was referring to the fact that he couldn't give Mary Communion since he was not Catholic, and they were not married.

As I walked through the cemetery, I silently thanked my father for being with me at all times.

NORMA AND JOE

NORMA

Judy launched into a monologue when I said, "Hello."

"Joe needs a volunteer. It's for his wife, Norma. He needs to get out of the house. She can't be left alone, and they agreed to have a volunteer visitor, once a week for an hour. Someone upbeat, cheerful, and absolutely will NOT talk about hospice or dying. You will be PERFECT, and the best part is they live across town from you. I told him to expect you at one o'clock on Thursday. I hope that's okay."

Joe opened the door, smiling. "Judy said you would be

prompt." He shook my hand and ushered me into the living room. Joe was a head taller than me, clean-shaven, with thick salt-and-pepper hair in need of cutting. He was thin and healthy-looking. His faded jeans and long sleeve button-down shirt were clean. Norma used to cut Joe's hair. The fact that she could no longer do it was the primary reason she agreed to have a volunteer visitor. Joe needed a haircut.

"This is my wife, Norma," Joe pointed to a frail woman with a smile to match his. She was sitting on the far end of the sofa, wearing jeans, a T-shirt, and house slippers. A towel-like turban covered her bald head. I smiled back. We had an immediate connection.

Joe indicated for me to sit at the end of a second sofa along the wall to the left and at a right angle to where Norma sat. Joe sat at the end of the living room, ten feet away, directly opposite Norma, in a wing chair, with an ottoman. We spent the afternoon getting acquainted.

I learned that they enjoy traveling. Joe was a civil engineer. They were both Italian and opinionated. They had three adult children. All were married. Jack, the oldest, had a daughter, Kirstin, the only grandchild, a senior in high school. Joe and Norma had moved to Steilacoom to be close to Jack and his family. The other two children, Mark and Lesley, lived out of state. Both were married, neither had children.

Steilacoom is a small town where there is a palpable tension between the "old timers" and "newcomers." The old timers, whose grandparents and great-grandparents founded Steilacoom, live in the original middle section of town above Main Street which parallels the shoreline of Puget Sound.

The "newcomers" live in two subdivisions: one on the east, the other on the southwest side of town. Joe and Norma were unusual. They were relative newcomers who lived in an older neighborhood in the midtown residential area.

When Joe and Norma decided to move closer to Jack, they admitted they had little in common with the "Steilacoom Settlers," as they called their neighbors.

Norma and Joe enjoyed attending horse races, traveling from one race to another until Norma no longer had the health or stamina to do it.

Norma said, "My brother and I are close, but I don't have much contact with my sisters."

From that first visit, Joe established a routine. The three of us would sit in the living room, exchanging greetings and pleasantries, the weather, and news about town. Sometimes, we chatted for ten minutes. Then Joe would stand abruptly and say, "I need to be going."

Before saying goodbye to Norma, he would address me, "I'll be back in an hour." He always was. From his chair at the end of the living room, he would pass the dining table, go through the galley kitchen, and into the foyer. Then, as he went out the front door, he would call out, "I'll see you later, honey!" Sometimes, he would turn around, walk into the living room, behind the sofa, smile down at Norma, and kiss her on the cheek before he left.

As soon as the door shut behind Joe, Norma would sit taller, turn toward me with her full attention and ask, "So, what is new?"

If I asked how it was going with her, she always said, "I don't want to talk about me. I want to know what's new with you."

Steilacoom has one small business area with a post office, liquor store, and a hairdresser. Across the street, there is a town hall with meeting rooms, tennis courts and Bair Drugs (which is also a café).

Norma always wanted all the details. I would begin from where I left off the previous week with tales and details of my experiences dealing with people in my job as a real estate agent. She would listen attentively, nod and smile. Sometimes commiserate, other times she'd offer an opinion regarding what I should or might do.

"Who did you see at the post office? Who was going in or coming out of the liquor store? Did you get your hair done? What happened at the last town hall meeting?"

I am a "mind-my-own-business" type of person. Despite living in Steilacoom several years, I was too new to know many residents to talk about. The town hall meetings were a different story. There were always contentious battles and arguments which divided the newcomers who wanted to see growth in small business, and the old timers who wanted things left just the way they were. It is a charming, historic town which has not changed much since it was founded in the 1800s. It claimed many firsts: first jail, first church, first school in the county, territory, or state.

Town hall meetings began promptly at seven o'clock and often ran past adjournment which was scheduled to be 9 pm. Often meetings ran until midnight or later. When that happened, I would stay until the bitter end, just to have stories to tell Norma.

After I answered all of Norma's questions about who I saw doing what, when, and where, I moved on to "adventures in real estate." She always remembered where our conversation ended the previous week. (At the time, I was working with my husband, Bob, in real estate while taking a break from nursing.)

"Did Cathy's house sell yet?" Norma wanted to know. Cathy, a single mom with three young children, had agreed to buy a house from her boyfriend's mother. I knew Cathy from working at Western State Hospital where she was a technician.

Cathy told me, "My boyfriend ditched me. I don't want to have anything to do with him or his mother! I want you to sell the house, I still owe her money!"

I listed the house a week ago. Norma was anxious for an update. The property was zoned for commercial use, making it attractive to investors. However, the interior was in such poor condition that it was a "tear down."

I stopped by the property on the way to visit Norma. There were six business cards from agents who had shown the property. Holes had been poked in walls and ceilings to find out how much insulation was there. Much to my surprise, I also found a friend of Cathy's camping out with her two children while babysitting Cathy's three. We were both relieved when they moved into an apartment and the house sold a week later.

After hearing all of this, Norma commented, "It's better than a soap opera!"

The next week, the doorbell rang in the middle of "adventures in real estate." Norma said, "I'm not expecting anyone."

I answered the door and found a short, chubby woman wearing blue scrubs, carrying a black bag with the Franciscan Hospice logo staring at me.

She said, "I'm the hospice nurse to visit Norma."

I pointed toward the living room.

The nurse swept by me as I said, "I'm RuthiE, the hospice volunteer. I visit on Thursdays."

I returned to my usual position on the sofa.

The nurse spoke to Norma, "I was scheduled to visit you yesterday but couldn't make it, so I came today. I hope that is OK."

Without waiting for Norma to respond, she took vital signs–blood pressure, pulse, and respirations. "Why do they call them vital signs?" Norma asked me later.

The nurse asked Norma questions in rapid succession. "Are you having any pain? How is your appetite? Are you moving your bowels?"

Annoyed, Norma gave one-word responses: "None. Fine. Yes."

Then, the nurse sat on a footstool with her back to me. She asked Norma some more personal questions that Norma and Joe had shared with me at our first meeting.

It occurred to me she might be meeting Norma for the first time.

"Excuse me," I finally said, "I can leave and come another day, Norma, if you wish."

"No!" Norma spoke up immediately and firmly. "I want you to stay, RuthiE!"

The hospice nurse left a few minutes later, and Norma and I picked up our conversation where we had left off.

When Joe came home, he asked, "How did it go?"

Norma reported grumpily, "The nurse came."

"Good," Joe said, "She couldn't come yesterday."

Norma raised her voice, "It's not good! She took up 15 minutes of my time with RuthiE."

I laughed. It warmed my heart to hear how much my visits meant to her.

I said, "Okay, Norma, I owe you 15 minutes. I promise I will make it up to you."

The next week, Joe brought home a very large burrito from Taco Bell because Norma mentioned she was hungry for one. Joe handed the burrito to Norma.

Norma looked at me and said, "Will you split this with me? It's big enough for the 'Jolly Green Giant.'"

Joe said, "RuthiE, I would have gotten one for you. I didn't know if you liked them."

I said, "I do like them, and I'd be happy to split this one with Norma."

From then on, Joe brought two regular size burritos. My arrival and Joe's departure were already ritual. My leaving also became a ritual. Norma and I enjoyed a burrito lunch at the end of every Thursday visit.

Several burrito lunches later, Norma became too weak to walk. Joe brought her to the living room in a wheelchair and parked alongside the sofa. I moved to the ottoman in front of Joe's chair. We were still 10 or 12 feet apart; however, I was now directly opposite Norma instead of off to her side. That was the week I gathered a bouquet of daffodils from my front yard and brought them to Norma.

"What did you do that for?" Norma asked disappointedly.

Joe explained, "Norma likes to see flowers growing in the yard, not cut."

"Why not?" I asked.

"They die," Norma said.

Without thinking, I blurted out, "Flowers bloom. They are beautiful, and then they fade and die. Just like people."

"Yes," Norma agreed. She looked at the floor instead of making eye contact with me.

My words were no sooner out of my mouth than I thought, "Oh my gawd!" Why did I say THAT! I'm not supposed to speak of death!"

Embarrassed by my blunder, I said, "I'm sorry, Norma."

I never brought her cut flowers again.

Norma did speak of death one time. She openly expressed her dismay at the suicide of a nephew. "How could a young person so full of life and health take their own life when …" She shrugged her shoulders with her hands upturned. The only sounds were the oxygen tubing connected to her nose and the machine that helped make it easier for her to breathe.

After Joe left that day, Norma tapped on the arms of the wheelchair and lamented, "It's just one more thing to give up."

Intuitively, I recognized she was referring to walking. In the Guided Imagery meditation of "our own death experience" in volunteer training, walking was one of the things we had to "give up." I sat in silence. I felt incredibly sad recognizing that Norma was really dying whether we talked about it or not. I could no longer pretend.

"I'm going to miss you," I said looking directly into her eyes.

"I'm going to miss you, too," her eyes met mine.

While tears streamed down our cheeks, we sat in silence for several long moments of deep connection.

Then, Norma grabbed a tissue from the box beside her, blew her nose, and said firmly, "That's enough of that!"

Joe called me a few days later, his voice calm, steady, and matter-of-fact.

"The nurse just left. She said Norma is regressing very quickly, and I should call the kids and her brother and tell them to come. I'd like you to be here, too."

When I arrived, Joe welcomed me and thanked me for coming. He said, "Make yourself at home," which I had always done vivaciously, anything to entertain Norma. However, that night felt different—reverent, tender. There was a gentleness that was palpable.

Simmering on the stove to the left of the front door was a large pot of spaghetti and another of homemade sauce. They were some of the best I'd ever eaten. As family members arrived, I served spaghetti in large flat noodle bowls to those who wanted some. No one sat at the table. Like the others, I ate standing up, only satiating hunger, not sharing the meal or small talk.

Norma's brother, Sonny, arrived a short time later. I had never met him or his wife, yet it felt perfectly normal to welcome them with a hug and kiss, as though we had known each other for years. He was as stout a man as Norma was slight.

I shall forever be grateful for the love I witnessed and shared that evening. Grateful that I could be with Norma and her family in her final hours. Norma was lying on the bed she and Joe shared. The room was softly lit. Norma was propped up with pillows behind her back and head. A pillow on either side of her torso for support in keeping her upright, making it easier for her to breathe. There was another pillow under her knees to keep her in the upright position. Family members were kneeling or seated around her bed. I was in the corner of the room at the foot of the bed. It was so quiet; a "church-like" silence. Norma's eyes were shut, her breathing even, neither fast nor slow.

Suddenly, Norma became agitated, struggling to sit more upright, trying to push the bed covering off with her hands, kicking with her feet. She tried to speak but her words were unintelligible. She responded to questions with mumbling and negative shakes of her head. It happened so quickly and suddenly–intuitively I asked, "Norma, do you have to pee?"

She nodded her head vigorously, YES. The room emptied

quickly while I helped Joe move the bedside commode next to the bed, together we gently lifted Norma, lowered her pajama bottoms, and sat her onto the commode. Joe stood behind her to hold her upright. Norma immediately voided a loud, long stream of urine. As it hit the bottom of the commode pan Joe said, "My gawd, Norma, you sound like a racehorse."

Norma smiled, eyes closed, leaning her right cheek against his arm.

We got Norma settled into the pillows, and the family resumed their places and prayers. Norma looked comfortable and at peace. I watched in fascination as her complexion slowly became sallow, pale, and yellowish, waxy in appearance as her organs shut down. Her body appeared to glow, reminding me of a melting candle.

Norma suddenly opened her eyes and looked around, startled. Taking in the whole room, she asked lucidly, "What time is it?"

"Eleven o'clock," several mourners answered in unison.

Looking in my direction, she asked, "Is RuthiE still here?"

"Yes, Norma, I'm still here."

She closed her eyes, and in a clear, soft voice said, "Well, you better go home now."

She was right. It was late. I had been there for six hours. I said, "I will leave in a little bit. Remember, I owe you 15 minutes? Norma, I'm giving it to you now."

Norma smiled without opening her eyes.

A short time later, perhaps 15 minutes, I felt a sense of peace with Norma, her family, and the space surrounding them. I kissed Norma's forehead, whispered goodbye, and slipped out of the house without disturbing the family vigil.

Norma's daughter, Lesley, called just before dawn and said, "Mom slipped away. It was so peaceful, like she was carried by gentle, loving angels." I hung up, feeling at peace. It was, as we say in hospice, "the expected outcome."

Months later, Judy shared a letter Sonny sent to Franciscan Hospice. *"I will never forget RuthiE Neilan. She greeted me like she was part of the family. The love, warmth, caring she showed those last hours were so sincere. I witnessed love, attention, assistance, given not only to Norma but to her husband, Joe, their three children, Jack, Mark, and Lesley, my wife, and me in the moments of our deepest sorrow. It has made an impression on me that will last forever.*

JOE

Joe's story did not end with Norma's death. I had an appointment to meet with a housing inspector the following morning. I was thinking of Norma as I led the way to the back of the house, the inspector following. As I rounded the house corner, a small branch hit my face. I raised my hand, caught the branch, snapped it off and almost tossed it aside when I recognized the blossoms. I was holding a small branch from a dogwood tree. I remembered the legend I had been taught.

The dogwood tree had once been as strong and large as an oak. Its wood was used to build the cross upon which Jesus was crucified. The small shrub held significant meaning with its tangled branches and the blossom brackets with red-tinged ends that represent a cross and nails. The center of the blossom is a tight cluster representing the crown of thorns worn on Christ's head. The dogwood blooms in early spring, coinciding with the Christian celebration of Easter.

A thought passed through my mind: *This is a symbol of the resurrection. Take it to Joe.* I went there directly after the inspection.

Lesley answered the door. I thrust the dogwood branch into the space between us. She said, "Oh, we don't want flowers for mom. We were just talking about that."

"These aren't for your mother. They're for Joe."

Lesley smiled and ushered me into the living room. The windows were shuttered, curtains drawn. The sun was shining at midday, indoor lights were on, yet the room was dark. Very dark.

Placing the dogwood branch on the square coffee table in front of Joe, the blossoms glowed a soft pink. I told the story of the Dogwood Legend.

Joe called me the next day. "Can we get some more dogwood?" In addition to flowers for the church, Joe purchased a number of dogwood-themed items–small clocks, vases, and plaques–as gifts for the hospice staff. In fact, I came home one day to find a small dogwood tree in a 5-gallon container. Joe helped me plant it in my front yard. Dogwood had become an anchor for Joe in his grief.

Six months after Norma's funeral, Joe spoke to a class of new hospice volunteers.

Of the dogwood, Joe said, "It started with a twig, then a few branches for the funeral, then a part of all of my possessions. It lets me dwell on the positive instead of the negative."

Peace with the Smiths

Judy spoke quickly, her sentences all running together. "RuthiE, I need you to go out to the Smiths, today. The RN case manager specifically asked for you. Mrs. Smith is in a coma, and the nurse doesn't know what is keeping her here. Her two daughters came from out of town. They don't get along and can't agree on how to take care of their mother. Mr. Smith isn't holding up."

When she paused, I asked "What did the case manager say, exactly?"

Judy said, "If she could just shake the sheets, Mrs. Smith would be gone."

("Shake the sheets" is an in-house expression that acknowledges an actively dying patient. It is a positive thought or desire to give the patient a boost into the waiting arms of angels. Many who work in hospice, including me, believe in angels and their assistance with dying.)

I was not surprised at Judy's call or request. I had been a hospice volunteer for several years by now. She trusted my observational skills and judgment. I did feel a little awkward about visiting since I had not met the patient or family. I called to let them know I would be stopping by at the request of their case manager.

Introducing myself as a volunteer with hospice, I sat with Mr. Smith at the kitchen table, explaining that I had come to see how things were going and if they needed anything. Mrs. Smith's hospital bed was directly in front of us in the middle of the living room, an arrangement that is typical in hospice at-home care.

One of the daughters acknowledged my presence with a curt nod, the other did not even look in my direction. I could feel the tension in the air as one daughter supported their mother onto her side while the other rubbed lotion onto her back, then snapped a fresh sheet in the air and let it float down to cover

Mrs. Smith's emaciated frame. The expression *Shake the sheets* came to my mind. Positioning Mrs. Smith with a pillow behind her back, another between her knees and a light blanket over the sheet, they glared at each other and at me and left the house.

Family members, especially adult children, are not always in agreement about the care their dying loved one receives. One might wish for more medication, the other less. One might encourage eating while the other honors the patient's refusal of food. I had no way of knowing what was going on between the two women or what was triggering their animosity toward each other.

I watched the women in silence and tried to focus on the belly breathing that I learned early in nurses' training. This "here-and-now" breathing triggered a relaxation response that kept me centered, calm, and shielded from the daughters' negative energy.

Looking exhausted, Mr. Smith sat next to me at the kitchen table with his eyes lowered.

Once we were alone, I asked, "How's it going?"

Early in hospice work, I was taught to ask, "How is it going?" instead of "How are you?" which tends to elicit an automatic response, "I'm fine." To ask, "How is it going?" offers awareness and interest in the current situation and allows space for an open-ended response. When asked, "How is it going?" a person is more likely to say, "It's up and down" or "not so good." Or, they may even offer more details. This was the case with Mr. Smith.

He spoke softly without looking at me. "I am so tired. I wish she would just go. I love her, but I am so tired. I just want it to be over." Tears welled up. He stood and mumbled, "Have to check on the mail," and he abruptly left the house.

It is not unusual for men to avoid expressing emotions, especially tears. Men are taught from an early age that crying is not appropriate and is out of character with male identity. How many times have we heard parents say, "Boys don't cry." This teaching carries over into adulthood. It did not surprise me that Mr. Smith's feeling of sadness was redirected into his abrupt departure. If any of his tears should fall, they would not be witnessed.

I was grateful for the opportunity to speak to Mrs. Smith alone. It is believed and taught that hearing is the last of the senses to go in the dying. The unresponsive patient can hear even though they cannot respond. I said a silent prayer as I approached Mrs. Smith's bed. I prayed, *please let me say the right words.* I leaned over the bed railing closest to Mrs. Smith's head. She looked at peace. Her eyes were closed, her breathing even and soft, her face relaxed.

I spoke to her in a normal voice. "Mrs. Smith, I'm RuthiE, a volunteer from hospice. It is okay to go. Your husband told me he is tired. He told me he loves you. He told me he wishes you would go." I paused for a moment, then continued, "Please don't worry. We will be here to help him. It is okay for you to go." I repeated, "Hospice will follow up with Mr. Smith after your death. It is okay for you to go."

There have been patients in the past who have expressed concern, usually from wives who have done all the cooking, cleaning, and housekeeping for their husband for many years. They worry about who will look after him—or how he will be able to look after himself. It is important to reassure the one who is dying, their spouse will be taken care of. Hospice is mandated by Medicare to follow up with bereavement care of the spouse for a full year following a patient's death.

I was still standing near Mrs. Smith's bedside when Mr. Smith returned from the mailbox, empty-handed. I told him I had spoken to his wife and told her he loved her and that the hospice team would be there to help him. And, that it was okay for her to go.

Mr. Smith swiped his hand across his face as if to erase his fatigue. He nodded his head slightly, reached out to shake my hand, and whispered, "Thank you." I left quietly, feeling new peace in the room.

Judy called the next day, "RuthiE, she died three hours after you left! What did you do?" I started to say, "Nothing," but realized, I should tell the truth. "I gave her permission to die."

It is important to remember that hearing is the last of our senses to go. Tell the patient they are loved and that those left behind will be looked after, and that it is okay to go.

It is.

JIM: A WINDOW IN TIME

"We are a licensed skilled nursing facility; he doesn't belong here. I am so glad you can take him for outings." Arlene, the social worker at Georgian House, ushered me through the open doorway of Jim's room simply stating, "Here he is. Jim, this is RuthiE from hospice."

Having delivered me to Jim's room, Arlene left quickly. I stood silently for a moment, the walls of Jim's room were the same stark white color as the hall, a patchwork quilt across the foot of his bed, and a couple of framed pictures on the wall made it less sterile. I was glad to notice the smell of disinfectant was gone.

Jim was fully dressed, lying partially on his left side crosswise on top of the covers, his head facing the door.

I pulled up a chair and introduced myself. "Hi, I'm RuthiE from hospice."

Jim responded, his speech so garbled, I could only nod, smile, and focus on his face, hoping to read his lips. I listened with my heart. This is a term and technique I first learned about in hospice. When a patient or family member has difficulty with verbal communication, they can often be understood by focused listening and observing how words are delivered as much as which words are being said. Jim's speech was extremely difficult to understand because of a cancerous growth in his esophagus complicated by his lack of dentures. His words garbled, bubbled, and ran together.

Except for my ability to piece together every third or fourth word, it would not have been a two-way conversation at all. His pain and anguish were quite clear as his jumble of words spilled out. He repeated, "Myfamilynevercomeslamalonelhavenoone. Myfamilynevercomeslamalonelhavenoone. Myfamilynevercomeslamalonelhavenoone." When I finally understood what he was saying, I protested. "That's not true! Now you have me."

Cynically, he raised his eyebrows, as if to say, "Oh, really? For how long?"

I told him I would come back and take him to church Sunday.

He looked directly into my eyes and garbled a readily understood, "Thankyou."

Jim wore a "Sunday Best" black suit which hung loose on his thin 5'8" frame. He told me later he wanted to wear it, "notjustatmyfuneral." His gray hair combed wet could not disguise the amateur haircut. His clean-shaven face could not hide the outdoor roughness of the homeless. He looked ill-at-ease which reminded me of my father who wore bib overalls all his life and was uncomfortable in a suit. I liked Jim immediately.

As I signed the "Visitor" book, required to take a patient out, I wondered aloud, "How long will we be gone?" An hour, I decided.

Jim mumbled, "Willtheyhavefellowshipafter?"

I replied, "Jim, I'm sorry, I'm not sure we can stay. I have an open house scheduled this afternoon for my broker."

Jim didn't reply.

We arrived at the church a few minutes before the 10 o'clock service. We were greeted by an usher and handed a bulletin. We found a place to sit halfway up the aisle on the left and slid into the center of the pew. I looked around the dimly lit sanctuary. The nave consisted of one main aisle down the middle of the cavernous space with an aisle on either side. The pews were sparsely populated. A small congregation for such a large space, I thought. Parishioners were middle-aged and middle class. They were well-dressed in suits and ties and dresses, reflecting the surrounding Lakewood community of older, well-kept homes.

Once the service began, the choir sang, and the pastor delivered a sermon based on Scripture. Then, he delivered a special announcement. "There is a gentleman at Georgian House who needs a ride to church."

This information was also written in the bulletin we held in our hands. I wanted to stand and say, "Look he is right here!"

Jim gave me a look. He shook his head emphatically, "NO!"

I remained silent because of the way he glared at me.

A long pause settled over the room. The pastor looked around. Papers and people rustled in the pews. No one volunteered. The service ended with the pastor's invitation, "Coffee and cookies will be served. Everyone is welcome."

We stepped into the vestibule to see a coffee urn and a platter of cookies. Responding to the look of longing on Jim's face, I said, "We can stay for a little bit if you'd like."

Jim smiled, nodded, and mumbled, "Yes."

People rushed us, drawn to my HOSPICE nametag badge. I suspect they were curious to find out who among them was in hospice care. They left as soon as I introduced Jim, again stating, "He needs a ride to church next week."

One parishioner said, "That's nice," as she walked away.

"Oh, I see ...," said another.

"I can't," said a third.

Only one parishioner stopped long enough to nibble a cookie. The rest of the congregation rushed out into the parking lot. I understood why they avoided refreshments after one sip of the insipid brown liquid and a bite of a stale cookie.

The host couple exchanged a glance and laughed nervously as Jim slurped his coffee, cooling it clumsily with water from the squeeze bottle he carried in his pocket. Jim nibbled, coughed, and sputtered into a paper napkin, turning his back when the woman standing next to him frowned. We left a short time later.

On the drive back to Georgian House, Jim said, "thepeopleweren'tfriendly. Didn'tlikethepreacher."

I agreed wholeheartedly.

Then he said, "thecookieswerethebest."

I disagreed, "I thought they were stale."

Jim responded, "MostIvehadtoeatlongtime."

"What!?" I asked, "Don't they feed you at Georgian House?"

Listening carefully, I heard Jim say, "theyfeedmethroughthistube." He patted his stomach. "Lookslikebabycrap."

I almost drove off the road! Had I understood correctly? Jim was not supposed to take anything by mouth?

I whined, "You are fed through a stomach tube? I let you have coffee and cookies! "What is the staff going to say?"

Jim conspired, "I'mnotgoingtosayanythingtothem."

When I dropped Jim off at Georgian House, he added "thestaffcanjustgotohellnoneoftheirdamnbusinesswhatIdoit'smylife!!"

Monday morning, I called Judy as soon as the hospice office opened, to deliver the required "after action" report. She barely said hello before I shouted, "Why didn't you TELL me Jim was NPO (nothing by mouth)?"

Judy replied, "What? Nobody told me he had this restriction." She sounded as shocked as I had been.

"I let him have coffee and cookies after church," I confessed, concerned because I had violated the doctor's order. Most people are familiar with the NPO order which a doctor gives prior to certain tests or procedures. It is also used when a person has difficulty swallowing and is fed formula through a tube inserted through the abdominal wall into the stomach which was the case with Jim. The reason for NPO orders for people with esophageal cancer is to avoid the risk of aspiration of fluid into the lungs which can cause pneumonia.

"Did you tell anyone?" Judy asked.

"No, only you," I said.

"And he's okay?"

"Seems to be fine. He actually liked the stale cookies. He said it wasn't any of the staff's business."

Judy and I agreed it would be our secret. If anyone asked, Jim had enjoyed himself on the outing to church, period. Since Jim and I hit it off, I agreed to be his weekly hospice volunteer visitor.

I arranged my next visit with Arlene who was to communicate with Jim. When I arrived, Jim had signed himself out. I was surprised and disappointed. Standing at the nurse's desk I said that I had an appointment with Jim. The charge nurse said, "As long as he signs the book with an estimated time of return, he is free to come and go." She had no idea where he had gone.

"Jim doesn't trust people," Arlene told me, waving her arms

around in her usual fashion. "He doesn't believe you are really going to come." She continued, "Jim had been found living in his car in a small town along the peninsula south of Puget Sound. He had been diagnosed with esophageal cancer and has a stomach tube to provide nourishment. Several social agencies cooperated to get him admitted to Georgian House and signed onto hospice. He was forced to sell his car in the process."

I was stunned to hear all of this.

Arlene continued, "He does have family, but they never visit. The nurses and I are so happy you are assigned to come every week. We will encourage him to keep your appointments," she said.

I thanked her and left after planning to come the following week. I came as promised, only to discover Jim had signed himself out again. I left a note: "Jim, I will come again next week. Hope to see you."

On week three, I was not surprised to see Jim's name in the "sign-out" book. Arlene said, "Jim made a point of telling me he would be at McDonald's having coffee if you'd bother to show up."

Show up! I'm the one who shows up every week. *Will he show up?*

Arlene continued "talking" with her hands. "Jim loves coffee.

He can't swallow, but he likes the ritual of holding the cup, the warmth, and the aroma." She waved her hands dramatically. "He was in AA (Alcoholics Anonymous) for years. After he stopped drinking booze, coffee and cigarettes became his new vices. Years later, he stopped smoking; and now, since the doctor ordered him NPO, we look the other way, as long as he has coffee away from the facility." I appreciated her trusting me with this information and almost told her about fellowship at the church. I felt less guilty about violating the NPO order since the staff was aware of his indulgences. I decided to track Jim down and join him for a cup of coffee.

I drove around the corner and down the street to McDonald's, parked, and went in to look around. I did not see Jim and turned to leave. Something, intuition I believe, urged me to look around again. I walked toward the back on the other side of the room. There, behind a row of artificial palm trees, elbows on the counter, cradling a cup of coffee, shoulders hunched over as if to hide, was Jim. I tapped his left shoulder as I slid onto the stool next to him.

His surprise gave way to a declaration, "WellTHEREyouare!" As if he had been waiting for me.

"Hi, Jim," I said, smiling. "Thought you could hide from me, eh?"

He grunted, "Hmmphhow'dyouknowIwashere?"

"The Social Worker told me." Jim gave me a lopsided grin as if pleased with Arlene for delivering his message.

"Jim," I said gently, "having a visitor from hospice is not a requirement; if you don't want me to come every week, it's okay."

After that, Jim was always ready and waiting for me; sometimes in the lobby, sometimes in his room. Jim was clearly higher functioning than the other residents. He found them "stupid" and "annoying." He often became impatient at overtures of friendship or conversation. He especially disliked those who had to use wheelchairs. On more than one occasion, he roughly pushed someone out of his way. Consequently, he would be sent to his room for "time out."

One week, when I arrived, he was sucking on a piece of hard candy from "theheavysetone," as he called Arlene. "Thisstufftasteslikeshit," he said, as we walked to my car.

"Why are you eating it then?"

"JustlookingforaplacetospititifanyonehappenstooffermesomeicecreamorcoffeeIwouldtakethat."

"Well, which is it?" I asked, handing him a tissue to spit the candy into.

"Coffee," he replied.

It was autumn, the season that the leaves change colors. I drove west, down the hill from Georgian House, through the famed "canopy of vibrant trees," into Steilacoom. Turning right, I drove along Chambers Bay, past the pulp mill, up through University Place where all the trees were especially bright and colorful. Jim oohed and ahhed and said, "I'dliketocomeback-nextspringandseeitgreen."

Jim received money from an unknown source. He never told me if it was social security or a veteran benefit. Nevertheless, he always had a few dollars in his pocket and always insisted on paying his share of the bill whenever we went out. I was heading to a specialty coffee house, the kind with a menu on a wall behind the display counter full of pastries. Jim had never heard of a coffee menu. He ordered a cup, black, the way he liked it, then found it too strong without cream. Jim voiced his opinion, "severaldollarsforcoffeeherewhenyoucanbuyacupatMcDonald's foronedollarisridiculous."

On our way out, having discussed the pros and cons of McDonald's versus "designer" coffee, Jim tripped on a small step. He stumbled, catching his balance before he fell. He spoke to the young waitress, "Itsureishellbeingoldliving-withcancer."

She gave both of us a puzzled look. "Excuse me, what?"

I could, by this time, easily understand his garbled speech. I looked her in the eye, slowly and clearly repeating, "He said, 'it-is-hell-being-old-and living-with cancer.'" Jim was clearly embarrassed by his outburst as the clerk was apologetic. We left and Jim mumbled, "Thankyou," on the way to the car. We never went back there.

Each time we returned from an outing Jim had an elaborate fabrication for the staff. We went to a bar for whiskey, another time it was beer, to a café for burger and fries or a milkshake with whipped cream. I never knew what Jim was going to say or what the staff thought. They rarely paid attention. I did worry from time to time we might get in trouble with the staff, or heaven forbid, the State Board of Nursing. If someone decided to follow up or investigate exactly what we did or where we went, it could mean trouble.

One week, Jim said, "IwanttoshopatTarget."

He had lost weight and wanted new pants, or maybe just a belt to hold up the pair he wore. Jim was unsteady, so we linked arms as we made our way through the store. I usually wore Birkenstock sandals, but that day, I looked down, surprised and embarrassed, to see I put on mismatched shoes in my haste that morning.

"Look Jim, I'm wearing one brown and one blue sandal. Bet you think I did it on purpose to entertain you."

Jim said, "Nopebetyouhaveanotherpairjustlikethemathome."

I appreciated his sense of humor which I had not encountered before.

Jim decided he could live without the belt and wanted a watch instead. We looked at watches beneath a glass countertop. He found several he felt he could afford. Before he took his hand out of his pocket to pay, he grumbled "Nahnotgoingtogetone."

I asked, "Why not?"

Jim shrugged, "Don'thavetotelltimewhereI'mgoing."

Our next visit landed on the day before Thanksgiving. Georgian House was filled with the delicious aroma of turkey and stuffing. Jim lamented "Theywon'tevengivemeataste." I felt a rush of sadness come over me at the cruelty of this situation. Wondering why they couldn't just let him lick a spoon or rinse his mouth with thin gravy and spit it out.

I asked, "Where do you want to go?"

Jim replied, "Anywhereoutofhere."

I asked, "What would you like to do?"

He responded, "Iwoulddieforsomemashedpotatoesandgravy."

I had been with Jim week after week as he slurped coffee. He had not once aspirated. I said, "Okay, let's go!"

I drove to the Lakewood Bar & Grill. This old-fashioned café with booths and red vinyl stools at a counter was staffed by a middle-aged waitress who knew I was a hospice volunteer and had accommodated my requests on a prior visit. After being greeted, I requested to sit as far as possible from the two occupied booths. We looked at menus.

Jim said, "Justcoffeeplease."

I ordered a cup of tea and reminded Jim of his earlier wish.

He grinned, "Andasmalldishofmashedpotatoeswithgravy-lotsofgravy."

I repeated his order to the waitress, adding, "With lots of extra napkins please," explaining, "He will cough a lot."

Despite knowing that Jim could not swallow, I was not prepared for the varied sounds of choking, coughing, and spitting. I had to look away to cover my reflective gag response, as each mouthful came back with noise and mucus.

I asked for more napkins. Reassuring the waitress who had a frightened look on her face. "He is okay. I am a registered nurse. Really, everything is okay."

She retreated to a distance but continued to keep an eye on us.

Jim polished off the small dish, pushing it away with a satisfied grin. All the contents spit into the wad of napkins the size of a football on the table in front of him. "Thatwasthebestdamnedmashedpotatoesandgravylhaveeverhadinmywholelife."

We said goodbye to the waitress and left a very large tip.

As the Christmas season approached, Jim told me, "Thissmyfavoritetimeoftheyear."

I was able to score free tickets to the Baptist Church's "Singing Christmas Tree," a staged song-and-dance extravaganza performed on tiers of risers in a tree shape. I was both impressed with the talent displayed and surprised to hear Jim's grumbling.

"Itwasdisappointingtheydidn'tsingmyfavoritesong."

"What is your favorite song?"

"JingleBells," he said with the voice of a sad little boy.

On the way back to Georgian House, I drove through several neighborhoods with light displays which cheered him up.

On Christmas Day, Bob and I arranged to bring Jim to our

house for the afternoon. I told him, "I have a 15-inch-tall, stuffed toy pig that sits on its hind quarters and wears a Santa hat."

When we got home, I handed the pig to Jim and directed him. "Squeeze the toes on his left foot."

To Jim's delight, the pig makes oinking sounds to the tune and rhythm of "Jingle Bells." *Oink-oink-oink.*

Jim played it twice, smiling the first time, and throwing back his head and laughing out loud the second time, when he recognized the melody of his favorite Christmas song. I'd never heard Jim laugh before. It was beautiful. We gave him a cassette tape of "Jingle Bells" before taking him back to Georgian House. With moist eyes, he said, "ThankyouforbestChristmasever."

Shortly after Christmas, he said, "Iwanttobuymycoffin."

I was not looking forward to this in the least.

I took Jim to Evergreen Mortuary, recommended by Arlene. It was raining, and we sloshed from the car to the mortuary entrance.

The crappy weather did not disturb Jim at all. "It'sgoodtobeout."

I considered the alternative and agreed. We went inside, and I introduced myself to the young man at the front desk who looked barely old enough to shave. Before I could explain our purpose, Jim took my arm, shook his head "no" and stepped forward. The young man looked from Jim to me, and back to Jim.

Jim stood taller, squared his shoulders, and without emotion, said, "Iamheretobuymycoffin." He had to repeat himself two more times before the young man understood. To the clerk's credit, he did not ask for my help, and to Jim's credit, he did not lose his temper.

The young man turned us over to an older, rotund man who ushered us into a room filled with coffins. From there, we went into a second room and then a third. As we went from one room to the next, the salesman pointed to each coffin, praising beauty, workmanship, quality, durability. It was apparent as we went, the coffins were progressively plainer, simpler, and lower-priced. Jim continued to shake his head "no." Jim had already said he was on an *extremely* limited budget, and he wanted a blue box, his favorite color. I finally asked, "Is there anything less expensive?"

We were directed around a corner into a much smaller room.

The salesman said, "This is the last room. These coffins are made of fiberboard. I call it 'pretend pine' covered with fabric. He said, "I will be out front, if you have questions."

Jim and I talked about the "boxes," as we walked among the modest choices. Suddenly Jim's face brightened, "Thisone!" he said, touching a light blue coffin with an embossed fabric covering. The price was $500. Jim asked to see the coffin lid closed, and the salesman folded the white ruffled fabric lining inside and closed the lid.

I remarked, "Look, Jim, they will tuck you in." We stared in silence for a moment, then Jim patted the coffin lid, looked at me with a satisfied nod and half smile. "I'llbelayingonmybackitsjustaplacetoputmyboneslwon'tbethere."

His Veteran status confirmed, he was assured next of kin listed at Georgian House would be given an American flag at his funeral service. Jim met with the mortuary director to arrange a payment schedule. He declined the option for a vault to protect the coffin "from moisture."

He firmly stated, "Idon'tneedavaulti'mjustgoingtoendupasbones."

Revisiting this experience, I remembered selecting a coffin

for our stillborn son in 1982. Bob and I were also ushered into a small private office in the Hospital PX. We were seated at a desk and handed a catalogue with a choice of infant-sized coffins. There were only three choices. The first was a slim, white rectangle with a flat top. It reminded us of Styrofoam picnic coolers used at the beach. It cost a little over $100. The second miniature coffin was embossed white fabric covering "pretend pine," similar to Jim's. It cost more than $200 but less than $400. The final choice was solid wood, polished to high "gloss" with a price tag of almost $1,000. Bob had asked me to choose the coffin I wanted. It was not difficult.

I'll be damned if we buried our baby in what looked like a beer cooler. I thought the $1,000 solid wood coffin was an extravagance we couldn't afford. The white embossed "pretend pine" would work just fine. As Jim noted, it was just a place to hold bones.

On the drive home from the mortuary, Jim and I talked about where people go after death.

Jim lamented, "I'mafraidtodieIhavehorribledreamsofdevilsandfireIthinkI'mgoingtobepunished."

I asked him, "Do you believe in God?"

He said, "YesthatswhyIwillbepunishedIhaven'tlivedaverygoodlife."

"I believe in the benevolence of the 'Jesus Loves me' God of my childhood. Ask forgiveness, and you will be forgiven."

He looked skeptical. "Doesitwork?"

"You have nothing to lose. You ask Jesus in your heart to forgive you for all your wrongdoings."

After thinking for a few moments, he said, "I'lldoit."

Jim never spoke of fears or nightmares again.

When I arrived at Georgian House in early January, the charge nurse told me Jim had fallen in the shower. He'd experienced chest pain thought to be angina. This was a crisis that Georgian House could not handle. He had been admitted to Madigan Army Hospital. Unlike the majority of hospice patients, Jim was "full code," which was an order to resuscitate if found unresponsive, without heartbeat or respirations. A person who has a DNR (Do Not Resuscitate) does not wish to receive CPR (cardiopulmonary resuscitation). In other words, "allow natural death."

I drove out to Madigan Army Hospital. Jim was surprised and happy to see me. Despite his desire for "nomoretreatment," I found him attached to IV, stomach, and oxygen tubing.

He said, "Idon'tknowwhytheyarebotheringI'mjustgoingtocheckoutandgointoaholeintheground!"

He was angry he had been brought to Madigan and was anxious to return home. "TheymightjustaswellletmegobackhometoGeorgianHouse."

Catching a glimpse of our window of time together closing in, I decided to tell Jim how I felt. "If you happen to check out before I get back next week, I want you to know I love you. I'm glad we met. Thank you for sharing your life with me."

Jim started to cry, silent tears rolling down his rugged face. Tears rolled down my face too.

He declared, "I'mNOTafraidIloveyoutoothankyouforhappymemoriesofourtimestogether."

Before leaving, I wanted to bless him. I said, "I usually sing this. Do you want me to sing?"

He closed his eyes as I sang.

"May the Blessings of God be upon you. The Blessings of the Father and the Son. And may the Spirit of Peace, the Spirit of Love, be with you all your days."

In the silence that followed, he whispered, "Thankyou."

Jim finally convinced the doctors at Madigan that he was serious about no more treatment. His actual words were he'd "rather have a stick of dynamite with a short fuse stuck up his ass" before he would agree to the spinal tap procedure they wanted to do.

He was discharged from Madigan and transferred to the VA hospital. He had developed a bleeding stress ulcer treated successfully with lavage, running ice-cold liquid into and out of the stomach by way of a nasal gastric tube. He was back at Georgian House the following week. Arlene called to say that Jim was upset and crying.

"Can you come by and see him?"

When I got there, I found Jim dressed, sitting in a wheelchair in front of a vending machine next to the nurse's desk. Arlene told me the tumors in Jim's chest were growing rapidly and had spread to his brain. He was not able to sign himself out to walk to the grocery store next door; he had to rely on the generosity and kindness of staff to let him use the vending machine. Most refused to help. After all, he was NPO.

Jim said, "TheymademesoangryIcried."

I helped him select a drink. Sherrie, his favorite LPN, came along to help him select a candy bar. Then Jim said "I'mtiredIwanttogotobedgoodbye."

Sherrie wheeled him to his room, and I left.

The next morning, Arlene called to say, "Jim is non-responsive. The doctor said send him to Madigan." The ambulance is on its way."

So was I.

Jim was lying on his bed, eyes closed. I said, "Jim, it's RuthiE. I'm here." His head moved in a slight nod of acknowledgment. He did not open his eyes or squeeze my hand. The paramedic asked me to wait in the hallway while they started an IV and oxygen.

I went to the nurses' station to talk to the charge nurse. Holding back tears, I asked, "Why are you doing this? He is dying. Why can't you let him die in peace?"

The charge nurse was also holding back tears. "I have no choice; he is full code."

That evening, I called Madigan to ask about Jim being admitted. When I called the next morning, the nurse told me, "Jim opened his eyes and cussed me out."

I drove out to the hospital and walked into Jim's room.

Upon seeing me, he muttered, "Herewegoagain."

I demanded, "Is this what you want?"

Jim responded, "NoIwanttogohometoGeorgianHouse."

"Jim, you have to tell your doctor."

Jim nodded with determination. "Iwill."

Three days later, Jim was back at Georgian House, and in a few days, he was weak but responsive. I sat by his bed and read Bible verses he requested between brief naps. The 23rd Psalm: "The Lord is my shepherd, I shall not want." 42nd Psalm: "As a deer longs for water, so my soul longs for you." 121st Psalm: "I lift mine eyes unto the hills. From where my help comes," a favorite psalm of my father's.

Jim was determined to stay at Georgian House to die. He did not want to be readmitted to the hospital, yet he continued to refuse to sign the DNR forms Arlene had prepared.

I got a frantic and emotional call from Arlene on Thursday. "Please, can you come? The doctor is transferring Jim back to Madigan. He's full code. He's declined to sign the papers again. We're not equipped to keep him alive. He can stay here to die but he HAS to sign the DNR. Jim trusts you."

I jumped into my car and risked getting a ticket for "failure to yield to an emergency vehicle." I literally raced ahead of the ambulance to Georgian House less than a mile away. Pulling into the parking lot moments ahead of the ambulance, I ran to Jim's room. Arlene was at his bedside with the DNR paperwork.

The charge nurse came in and said, "The ambulance crew is unloading a gurney. Unless Jim signs the DNR, I have no choice except to send him to Madigan."

I sat on the edge of Jim's bed. Arlene stood behind my right shoulder. The head of Jim's bed was elevated, his breathing shallow and ragged. He was receiving oxygen through a cannula in his nose.

I asked, "Jim, do you know who I am?"

He gasped, "Yes."

"Jim, the ambulance is here to take you to Madigan."

"Nohospital," he gasped.

"Jim," I took a deep breath and forced myself to slow down enough to calmly explain, "Georgian House has no choice."

Jim shook his head and said, "Nohospital."

Gently, but firmly, I asked, "Do you know you are dying?"

Jim took a labored breath, nodded, and said, "YesNOhospital."

"Jim, do you wish to stay here to die?"

He hesitated, then said, "YesNOhospital."

"Jim, you need to sign the Do Not Resuscitate paperwork if you want to stay here." I took the clipboard from Arlene and read the first line, then asked, "Do you understand?"

He nodded.

I read the next line, waiting for him to signal understanding.

When he nodded, I continued line by line. When all the lines had been read, and Jim indicated he understood with a head nod, I handed him the pen.

Arlene and I witnessed his scribbled signature, and Arlene fled the room, waving the DNR form at the ambulance crew waiting in the hall.

I stayed behind, grateful that his wish would be granted. I said, "It is a gift to die where you choose, surrounded by people who care about you."

Jim nodded.

"I love you," I said.

"Iloveyoutoo," he whispered.

I put my hand in his as he said, "thankyouforbeingmyfriend."

On Friday, Judy asked me to speak to the new class of volunteers. I never know what I am going to say at those things. I found myself speaking–then crying–as I told the class about Jim and where he was in this final part of his journey. "What a gift he has given me," I said.

I shared with the class, "My dad died of cancer in 1980. There was no hospice in his community. I had no support. I became a hospice volunteer to keep others from going through the incredibly difficult time I went through without the support of hospice."

Jim's health declined rapidly after that. He was confined to bed and there were no more trips out. One day, I brought a bouquet of flowers purchased next door at the grocery store. He was so pleased and humbled. "Nobodyevergavemeflowersbefore," he mumbled softly, eyes wide and moist, as if it was the most incredible thing anyone could have done for him.

I thought "you have GOT to be kidding! He is at the end of his LIFE, and this is the FIRST time anyone gave him flowers?" The following week, I saw a sign: Tulips, three pots for the price of one. Arms full, I marched into Jim's room. The flowers I had given him a week earlier were already dead and still in the vase on the bedside table. He had refused to let the staff throw them out. I lined three pots of bright red tulips on the "over the bed table" in front of him and threw the dead flowers away.

Instead of gratitude he grumbled, "Howcomeyoukeepbringingmeflowers?"

"Because I'm not going to bring them to you after you're dead!"

Jim shot back, "GoodIwon'tneedthemthen!"

I softened. "Jim, I'm going to plant red tulip bulbs this fall to remember you when they bloom next year.

He looked me straight in the eye, "Thankyou."

We sat in silence as I remembered our precarious beginning which had developed into a trusted bond. We shared secrets and honesty. "Jim, thank you for letting me visit you these past months."

He responded, "Ilikedgoingoutwecan'tgoanywherewhydoyouwantocomesitwithme?"

I told Jim the truth. "You remind me of my father who died of cancer ten years ago. He was sick for months. He didn't ask me to come home until he was bedbound. Then a few weeks later, he told me it was time to go home, and he died after I had left. Being with you is kind of like being with my father."

Jim didn't say anything for several long minutes then asked "Areyoureallygoingtoplantredtulipsinmemoryofme?"

"Yes, Jim, I really will."

I visited Jim late in the afternoon where I found him lying on his back, right arm outstretched, his hand holding two tickets to the Seattle Sea Hawks. He told me his hospice nurse promised to take him to a game that weekend. He had looked forward to this outing for months. Now he was too sick to go. "Is there anything I can do for you?" I asked him on the last afternoon of his life.

He whispered, "Iwantrootbeer."

I stopped at the front desk to speak to the charge nurse, "I'm going next door to get a can of root beer for Jim."

She did not look up from her charting. "He is NPO," she said.

"I know. He is also dying, and he wants root beer. I am going to give it to him. Please have someone standing by with a suction machine."

When I returned, Sherrie, the licensed practical nurse (LPN) who loved Jim as much as I did, was waiting outside his room. She had a suction machine on wheels. Jim was no longer strong enough to suck on the straw. I held my fingertip to the top end of the straw which created a vacuum when put into the root beer which allowed liquid to be drawn into the bottom of the straw. Placing the straw between Jim's lips allowed the sweet liquid to release into his mouth when I removed my fingertip.

Jim managed to say, "Tastessogood," before he began to choke.

Sherrie suctioned while I created the vacuum in the straw,

and Jim sipped more root beer. Sherrie suctioned when he choked. The root beer helped loosen the thick secretions Jim could no longer manage. We continued the "sip, choke, suction" until Jim raised his hand to signal "STOP!"

Over the last few weeks, every time I saw Jim, I said goodbye as if it was for the last time. That day, with his deep sigh and the weary look in his eyes, I knew it would be the last time. I said my final goodbye to Jim, and as I left, Sherrie told me, "I will sit with him at 11 when I get off shift." I cried all the way home. Sherrie called a few minutes after midnight to say, "Jim died peacefully."

I never met Jim's hospice nurse, but she called to thank me for being a faithful volunteer and for getting him to sign the DNR. She also shared with me that she had met several of Jim's family members that morning. She witnessed them arguing over his meager belongings in front of him. Jim was too weak to resist or intervene.

"I kicked them out," she said.

We all shared an aversion for those who claimed to be Jim's family but never visited him until the day he died. None of us wanted anything to do with them and none of us went to the funeral.

A few weeks after Jim's funeral, I stepped outside, onto my back deck, into the cold, clear night. I looked at the sky full of stars. "Jim, are you okay?" I whispered. "Please let me know you are okay." I listened to the silence. Then, from behind, a single wind chime "DING" sounded like a small Christmas bell. I had an image of angels rushing straight up to Heaven. I knew Jim was okay.

As promised, tulip bulbs were planted that fall and bloomed after a late spring storm. Three red blooms waved bravely above the snow. I watched a deer come out of the woods and ravenously eat them, leaving only decapitated stems. I laughed. That brazen deer was a welcome reminder of defiant Jim.

BRIAN

Celebrating a wedding anniversary followed by planning one's funeral might seem bizarre to most people. It is perfectly normal in hospice care. Patients and families are encouraged to "tie up loose ends" and "plan for the future." For someone facing imminent death, the future includes a funeral. I have known patients to plan their memorial to include a starting time, hymns for soloist or congregation, and who will read the obituary. Prayers and scriptures selected by the one for whom the memorial is celebrated. Maria and Brian would plan Brian's funeral together. Brian was on "in-home" hospice because he had glioblastoma, an aggressive form of brain cancer.

Judy asked me to visit them and see how I could help.

When I arrived, Kelly, a lovely young brunette with a sullen expression had gone to her bedroom and closed the door. She took Evan, her 3-year-old stepbrother, with her. Her job was to keep him entertained during my visit.

Brian and Maria were freely communicating their love, anger, and concerns about Maria's rebellious 13-year-old daughter, Kelly. However, they were not speaking directly to one another. Maria sat on the sofa next to my right. Brian was in an armchair facing us on my left.

Maria said, "She is the spitting image of that jerk I divorced. I can't stand to look at her!"

Brian said," Please don't say that. She might hear."

Maria turned her back.

I realized I was serving as a conduit to their conversation. I stated, "You do realize, you should be talking to each other. Can you try to speak directly to each other?"

Maria turned to me, "No. This is the first time Brian and I have talked about Kelly without screaming and shouting at each other."

Brian nodded in agreement.

They enjoyed talking to each other with me as a buffer and asked if I could come again." With Judy's approval, we agreed I would visit on Thursday, the next week.

I was the logical volunteer to be assigned to them. I lived in Steilacoom on the other side of town. Maria and Brian lived on the east side, just off Steilacoom Blvd, a road I drove daily to and from work as an agent in real estate at Century 21.

My nursing background gave me knowledge and insight into Brian's diagnosis of glioblastoma. A patient's behavior can change dramatically from walking and talking one day to non-responsive the next. My age and life experience were also an advantage in dealing with a volatile teenager and a loveable preschooler.

Brian and Maria wanted to go out to lunch to celebrate their wedding anniversary, then stop at the mortuary and plan for Brian's funeral. At Maria and Brian's request, I took their young son, Evan, home with me for the afternoon. He played quietly stacking blocks. When I took Evan back home, his parents reported they had a lovely lunch and successful meeting with the funeral director.

On Monday the following week, I thought of Maria and Brian as I drove up Steilacoom Blvd past the turnoff to their house. "Maybe I should drop in," I thought. My next thought was, "No, I will see them Thursday." The same notion popped into my mind on my way to work Tuesday, and again on Wednesday. I shrugged it off both times.

On Thursday, I drove to Brian and Maria's house as scheduled.

Maria answered my knock with a quizzical expression, "Didn't they tell you?"

"Tell me what?"

"Brian died last night. He'd been saying he just wanted to live until his 38th birthday. We went out to dinner to celebrate. When we got home, he said he was tired and went to bed. He didn't wake up this morning."

I was completely stunned, shocked, and deeply sorrowful. I thought of Maria and Brian three days in a row and could have stopped for a spur-of-the-moment visit. I had ignored my inner wisdom.

With tears in my eyes and stricken with guilt, I told Maria, "I am so sorry I did not follow my intuition." Intuition is a sense of "knowing" without knowing HOW you know. It's a feeling in your gut.

I have since learned to trust that "knowing," no matter how strange, or illogical it might seem. Now, whenever a name or thought pops into mind, seemingly out-of-the blue, I now understand that it is a nudge from Spirit, and I must act on it.

Decades after that experience with Brian, I woke one

morning with a sharp, intense pain in my right side. I called my doctor. I "knew" with absolute certainty, what I needed was to speak to a grief counselor.

By this time, I had worked six months at Casa Hospice in Tucson as a registered nurse (RN) case manager. The case manager oversees the team (social workers, chaplains, bath aids, etc.) to provide care for a caseload of patients and families. I found the ongoing admissions and discharges emotionally difficult. I needed more time to release one patient before I welcomed another. Each admission brought anticipatory grief while still grieving the loss of the patient who had just expired or was about to die.

Faye, my supervisor, empathized. She said I had to learn to deal with this ongoing reality as a case manager. Ironically, the timing coincided with the one-year death anniversaries of my father-in-law, my flute-maker friend, Hawk, and Linda, my daily walking partner. Their dying within weeks of one another the previous year weighed heavily on my heart.

I was referred to Rajulia, an experienced grief counselor. Agnes, RN, the co-founder of Casa de la Luz, granted me a three-moth leave of absence. Remembering and reliving the last days of my involvement with family and friends helped to resolve the feelings of sadness surrounding the anniversaries of their deaths. I still needed to grieve past losses, including the stillbirth of our son, John Matthew, in Hawai'i. I recalled the overwhelming sorrow Bob and I shared the night he was born and the painful following days leading up to his funeral.

Grief issues surrounding case management were also resolved. My new assignment is that I would work weekends on call. Responding to specific needs of patient/families without the ongoing contact which would no longer overwhelm me. This is the position I held until I retired from nursing.

Bob received orders a short time after our son's death, and we moved to a new community. We never shared our sorrow with this community or with communities in three subsequent moves. Twenty years had passed since our baby's death. I tearfully confessed to Rajulia that Bob and I had never spoken of our stillborn son during all those years. I had blocked his loss from my mind but never from my heart.

Bob agreed to come to a session with me. I sat in my usual armchair with Bob on my right. Rujulia positioned herself in front of and between us. I recognized I had been sitting in the position of therapist when I was with Maria and Brian, coaching and encouraging them to speak to one another just as I was now being coached to speak directly to Bob.

I understand now what I didn't understand then. Speaking to the therapist was safe. Speaking directly to a loved one about an emotional topic is to risk vulnerability. I said I didn't think Bob grieved for our son after he was buried. Bob said he had not shared his sadness because he was concerned it would further upset me. I externalized feelings while Bob held his in. With Rujulia's guidance and coaching, we were able to speak directly to one another about our loss. To this day, we continue to do so.

The loss of a loved one is permanent, and grief is also permanent. Sharp edges of a stone tumbling into a stream will, overtime, become a smooth river rock. But it is still a rock. We will always speak of our small plot of land where our son is buried in Hawai'i. We remember him with sadness and a smile.

FINDING MY OTHER VOICE

Having grown up on the Flathead reservation in Montana, I readily joined the auxiliary in support of Steilacoom tribe's efforts and mission. I enjoyed the "For Members Only" privilege and looked forward to the program on Native American flute by Raven, a Cherokee.

I felt my excitement whenever I glanced the entry sign, "For members only." Joan, matriarch of the Steilacoom tribe and manager of the Tribal Museum, offered programs to auxiliary members whose membership provided financial support to the museum. The tribe purchased a "deactivated" church on Main

Street and turned it into a museum with a life-size diorama of early tribal life.

The NAF (Native American flute) program was held on the lower level of the museum. The brief sounds I heard of the flute haunted me as I entered the event. I wanted to hear more, but I couldn't stay for the entire program. I begged Joan to repeat the program so I could have a "do-over." A year later when Raven returned, I arrived early and stayed late. As I left the house, I told Bob, "I'm coming home with a flute."

Raven was a slender, 5'6" man. He was dressed in tan-colored buckskin pants and a shirt with fringe at the hem and beaded moccasins. His long, dark hair pulled into a ponytail at the nape of his neck was just past his shoulders. He invited us to sit with him in a circle on the floor. A multigenerational group of eight joined him in respectful silence.

Native American flutes were laid out like the spokes of a wheel. They rested on a fragrant blanket of fresh cut cedar branches which held the scent of the pungent smoke from a smudging bundle of sage.

Raven's voice was soft but authoritarian. He welcomed us and started with, "The traditional manner is to learn by watching and listening, do not ask questions." He paused then looked around the circle making eye contact with each of us before firmly stating, "If you pick up the flute, it will change your life."

The first time I heard this declaration, I was curious and excited and so grateful for the opportunity to participate. I listened intently as Raven said, "The cedar tree is sacred. It is a living being. The flute maker removes the heart of the tree in making the flute. It is your *responsibility* to put the heart back in with your breath. I was struck by his use of the term "response-ability." WOW! It is my *responsibility.* This declaration has stayed with me to this very day. Every time I breathe into the flute, I am conscious to play with my heart.

Raven invited us to pick up a flute. "Hold it lightly, with no more pressure than you would holding a baby's arm." He demonstrated bringing the narrow end of the flute to his mouth. "Breathe into it gently like a whisper," he said. The flutes have six holes he covered with his index, middle, and ring fingers; left hand on the top three holes and right hand on the bottom three holes. "Notes will change as you lift each finger," he said, demonstrating and lifting each finger in turn from the bottom to the top, except for the ring finger on his left hand, which I noticed remained on the flute. I later asked why, and he said, "Good question."

He elaborated, "It was Tom, maker of the flute, who told me

it is believed keeping the left-hand ring finger on the flute connects the flute to the player's heart."

In unison and then in turn, we played tentative sounds. There was much squeaking and squawking, none sounded remotely as smooth and lovely as Raven's demonstration.

At the evening's conclusion, Raven said, "There are lessons for you to learn. Let the flute teach you."

There were not enough flutes on the blanket of cedar branches for everyone. We were asked to choose the flute we felt drawn to without thought or examination. The flute that chose me was in a box delivered by flute maker Tom Stewart, of Stellar flutes. He had driven over from the coast and was ushered in by Joan. Standing next to Joan, I peered into the box, then reached in, selecting a flute as had been suggested, picking up the one I felt drawn to without giving thought to reasons.

I took the flute I had been drawn to out of the box. It was indistinguishable from the others except for a red and black thread wrap that glowed like a beacon in the darkened room.

I showed the flute to Tom who said, "This flute was made of yew, a scrub tree; ugly on the outside, beautiful on the inside. Sacred to the Druids in ancient times and the bark is harvested for cancer treatment in modern times."

When Tom said, *"made of yew,"* I thought he said, "*This flute was* made *FOR you,* ugly on the outside." I felt tears sting in my eyes. I felt insecure and like an outsider.

I said quietly, "What? You think I'm ugly?" We laughed together when Tom clarified he was speaking about the flute, not me. I told Tom, "I've always been interested in Druids and Celtic spirituality; I'm a nurse and a hospice volunteer." Tom smiled in his easy-going manner and said, "That's probably why this flute chose you."

The bird or block on top of this flute is a little duck shape; the red and black thread wrap, traditional colors of Pacific NW Native Americans, is in front of the duck. I felt a spiritual connection and sensed the duck was telling me, "I need eyes so I can see where we are going." With two pencil marks, I gave it sight. Although many flutes have passed through my hands, I have never parted with my first flute.

I brought my precious "Little Duck" flute home and repeated the fingering technique over and over with much squeaking and squawking. I learned the first lesson my flute had to teach me. I carried tension in my hands and shoulders. I felt frustrated attempting to play as I gripped the flute so hard, imprints from the flute's holes could be seen on my fingertips. I had to learn to "lighten up" and relax my grip. I felt like a dry sponge, wanting to soak up all I could from my new flute friend.

One afternoon while practicing the flute scales, a holographic image of my stern and critical high school band teacher appeared before me, slightly below eye level, in Technicolor. Although a miniaturized 2 ½ feet tall, he looked and sounded EXACTLY like the man who taught me clarinet decades earlier.

The apparition rapped his baton loudly on the music stand in front of him and shouted, "*You will NEVER get it right!*" and then disappeared. I had never experienced anything like that before. It surprised and frightened me, and I felt sick to my stomach. I put my flute away in its case and tucked it away in the corner of the room.

Every time I entered the room, I had to walk past the flute and could hear it whisper, "Pick me up and play. It's okay. You *can* do it." After several days, I relented. The flute taught me lesson number two: overcome self-doubt and fear and continue to practice every day.

I never knew, understood, nor can I explain what happened between me and the flute, but one day, months later, a crystal clear and beautiful fundamental note sang forth. This is the lowest note the flute is capable of playing. It is also the most difficult as all holes must be covered evenly to prevent air leaks. The sound resonated deep within my heart. It felt like hands grabbed my torso and literally tore my chest open. Healing tears gushed forth. I recognized a sudden release of emotion followed by peace and the warmth of love.

The flute taught me to be present to myself and to follow my breath, my mood, my heart. It taught me to *listen* to the sounds; one tone following another which is intuitive, not intellectual. When I was playing, it often felt like I was listening to someone else playing sounds that were being channeled from a universal source.

Playing the flute taught me to leave my ego at the door because the music I was playing was for the patients, their families, and the staff. I always asked audiences to please refrain from applause between songs, acknowledging that the applause would disturb the energy created by the flute.

While attending the first International Native American Flute Association (INAFA) convention in 2001, I had the opportunity to locate the memorial built to commemorate those who died there on May 4th, 1970. Students protesting the United States' involvement in Vietnam had been shot and killed by National

Guardsmen. I was dismayed to learn that part of the original site had been turned into a parking lot and a dormitory. The memorial, itself, was tucked away, out of sight, behind the dormitory.

I had a high G flute with me and thought to play a somber, mournful tune in memory of the dead. I put the flute to my lips, took a deep breath and exhaled. The horrific sounds: screeches, screams, cries, and shots I heard blasting out of it caught me off guard. It was as if someone else was breathing the heart back into the flute. Tears streamed down my face as I realized this was my heart still harboring anger and sorrow about my father's death being released through my flute. The flute was speaking my truth.

Chakra is a Sanskrit word meaning "wheel of light." Each of the seven chakras or energy centers in our bodies, has tones, vowels, musical notes, colors, organs, and nerve receptors associated with them.

Joan told me I was the only one in Steilacoom to continue with the flute after Raven's session and suggested I search online for other opportunities to learn. This search eventually led me to what I called the "flute camp circuit." It was similar to the powwow circuit many tribal and nontribal members take each summer. Going from one powwow to the next, I went to five flute camps in a single year.

The circuit began in June 1999 and ended in June 2000 at RNAF (Renaissance of the Native American Flute), founded by flute maker, Ken Light (Amon Olorin flutes), and R. Carlos Nakai, noted flute player. RNAF was a weeklong retreat held at Feathered Pipe Ranch near Helena, Montana.

At that first camp, Carlos asked those who were new to the flute to connect with someone with experience and ask for their help. I met, and am still friends today, with Julia who suggested I continue practicing the basic scales until I could play the notes rapidly up and down and add a few improvised notes at the top of the scale without error.

At the beginning of the week, Carlos encouraged us to reflect on who we are and where we came from for us to know where we are going. Playing in recital at the end of the week was mandatory. Since playing the scale was the only thing I knew how to play, that is what I played. Following Julia's advice, I played scales up and down, faster and faster.

My ancestors are Scot-Irish, English, French, German, Swiss, and Spanish. According to family oral history, my first ancestors came to America on the Mayflower. In fact, one was swept overboard and rescued by the crew after he grabbed a rope trailing the ship. The last of my ancestors arrived in the 1800s.

I was overcome with emotion as I reflected on this. Each life was a thread in my tapestry that led to me growing up on the Flathead reservation. I marveled to think my ancestors met and married on this side of the ocean. I doubt any of them would have met, much less married, in what we called "The Old County," from whence they had come.

I rattled off ancestral litany at the recital to introduce "*The Gathering,*" my improvised composition. With no idea of what I was doing, I played the notes of the scale up and down as rapidly as I could, adding additional notes at the top. In my composition, I remembered a phrase of music from an old sea shanty, "What shall we do with a drunken sailor." Hearing and recognizing this familiar tune, I thought, "Wow, did I just play a real song?"

RNAF was total immersion, like a weeklong sound bath. Our day began wrapped in blankets, drinking coffee in the lodge, talking, and playing flute all day long. There were class-like sessions, delicious meals, hikes, a hot tub, a sweat lodge, and a recital at the end of the week. Although RNAF no longer meets, the friendships forged there were everlasting.

My self-imposed flute camp circuit included two camps in

California–the first with Dennis Sizemore, the second a host of "women-only" teachers at "Women of the Winds." I have little musical background and quickly realized I was way out of my league at the first California workshop. I didn't understand half of what Sizemore was talking about. However, I enjoyed the company of flute players I met at RNAF in Helena.

One evening, sitting in the hot tub, Julia commented how sweet my husband, Bob, was for driving me from Washington to California for the flute camp. She suggested I write a song for him. Then, in the next moment, we both voiced the same notes, and in unison, sang, "*My Sweet Bob.*" It was the first song I composed. The moniker stuck, and all these years later, I still refer to him as MSB–my sweet Bob.

The second "all women" camp in California was much more my speed. We had sessions on self-hypnosis to overcome stage fright, learned how to tabulate notes, and how to "write" music. From these lessons, I became more comfortable playing music with and for others.

After the two camps in California, I planned to go to Seattle for a workshop called "Playing from the Inside Out," led by flute makers Hawk and Geri Littlejohn. After a beginner's first flute, usually in a key of G or F#, the logical progression was to get a flute in the key of A or key of E, above and below their original flute key.

As I recall, the premise was more flutes than more flute songs. Undecided whether to go higher or lower, I decided on both. I ordered a key of A flute from Scott Loomis in Oregon and a key of E from Hawk and Geri in North Carolina.

The A flute came first, and because it is shorter than the G, I gravitated to the A which is easier to play. Scott called to ask what I thought. He was especially pleased with the variation of color and pattern in wood grain. I did not fully appreciate the beauty of this flute until after we moved to Arizona. I called to let him know.

As I waited and waited for my Hawk Littlejohn key of E flute to arrive, my impatience got the best of me. I called to ask, "Where is it?"

Geri answered, "Isn't it there? I thought you called to say it came and how much you love it."

"No," I said. "I called because it's not here."

Geri said, "Well, go watch for it then."

I thought what a strange remark.

I said, "Okay," and hung up. I walked to the front window with a view of the cluster mailboxes at the bottom of the hill. I watched as a Red-tailed Hawk circled in the sky above as the mail carrier pulled up with the "signature" triangle box used to ship a flute.

I retrieved my boxed E flute and ripped it open on top of the dining room table. I sucked in my breath at the beauty of the wooden flute inside. An inner voice told me "slow down." I paused, sat back, and took a deep breath.

I distinctly heard a clear, whispered voice. "Hello, I am Grandmother." Her wood is lightning-struck poplar, sacred to the Cherokee. Poplar, Geri told me, is a water-filled tree that grows high on a mountain and can continue to live after being "struck by the fire of God." When the tree is harvested, the discolored wood, dark instead of pale blonde, was considered undesirable by furniture makers in North Carolina while flute makers immediately "snatched" it up.

Grandmother's body is two-tone—half pale and half dark. She remains one of my favorites. When I play at flute circle, the MC will introduce us, "RuthiE and Grandmother."

The makers of Grandmother, Geri and Hawk, had an unusual May-December relationship. They were quite compatible despite the difference in age. Geri is Jewish and practices a Lakota faith. Hawk was a well-known, respected flute maker. Once a white man, he reinvented himself as a Cherokee. I loved them both. I use their flutes almost exclusively in my hospice work. After Hawk's death from cancer, Geri has continued to grow into her own person and has become a leader in flute communities.

Hawk and Geri were well known for their workshop, "If You Can Sing It, You Can Play It on the Flute," was a new concept at the time. They introduced this concept with Hawk's explanation of our relationship to the flute which is made from trees. In his opening remarks, he said:

> *"The tree comes to us in the form of the flute. Bringing with it all of the experience of the tree which lives in three worlds: the Below World where the roots extend and communicate with all the crawlies that live below; the Middle World where you and I live, and the tree communes with all two-legged and four-legged beings; and the Above World where the winged ones live and commune with the tree in its branches and the elements of the wind and rain and sun. The tree comes to us with much knowledge of these worlds. The tree has a Spirit which is*

translated into the Spirit of the flute when it ceases to be a tree and becomes a flute. We are Spirit just as the tree and the flute are Spirit. We will breathe our Spirit into the flute so its heart can be given a voice. To make this a strong, true, and loving voice, we must first connect to our own heart."

Raven, Hawk, and other flute makers teach that the heart of the tree has been removed in the making of the flute, and it is up to us to put the heart back into the flute with our breath.

It was at this camp, I woke one morning singing a chant I thought we had learned the previous evening. When I sang the chant for Geri, she said, "I've never heard that before in my life. It must have come from Spirit. This happens when we are open."

Puzzled, I continued to sing the chant, and was able to play the melody on my flute as Geri predicted. Several months passed, and sheet music surfaced of a tune I had written seventeen years ago while grieving my stillborn son, John Matthew. The chant, which had come to me with such clarity, was the same melody on this sheet music.

The last camp of the circuit, my second at RNAF, occurred in

2000. I received "most improved player" award. I realized the next flute camp I attended would be one I facilitated. This came to pass several years later. In the meantime, I continued to use the flute as my "other voice" as I'd been taught–to focus on breath and sound; to "sing" words into the flute. By focusing on what I was feeling, and thinking about what that emotion might sound like, I was able to "say" what I wanted to say with the flute.

Monthly hospice volunteer meetings were mandatory and began with "check-in." Each person was allotted less than three minutes to share feelings and activities of the previous month. There were always 25 to 30 members present. I chose to do "check-in" with my flute.

My feelings were generally calm and peaceful, articulated with three or four smooth, sustained notes. On the occasions I felt agitated and anxious the sounds would be a series of jagged shrieks. Other volunteers were startled at first. As time went on, they were accepting, understanding, and appreciative. After sharing "my other voice" at meetings for a year, Judy stopped me and said, "Michael has a patient at Puyallup SNF. Her name is Rebecca, and she likes music. Would you play for her? She has Huntington's chorea."

I was willing but petrified.

REBECCA

Huntington's chorea is a hereditary, uncurable, progressive disease characterized by severe, rapid, purposeless, involuntary movements. Because the Central Nervous System (CNS) is involved, articulation is difficult. And because this disease involves the brain, I did not know how sound and vibration would affect Rebecca's nervous system.

"This is Michael," a nurse said, pointing to the middle-aged man standing next to her. Michael, Rebecca's hospice nurse, was about 5'10" with a slight paunch, no stubble, and thick, coal-black hair combed only by running his hand through it. He looked clean but rumpled. He had on a plaid flannel shirt. The shirt was untucked from new denim jeans and ankle-top hiking boots. Unsmiling, his head was tilted, and his fingers were in his pockets. As he looked at me, I could see kindness in his eyes.

I said, "Yes, I'll play for her, but only if you'll be there." His eyes met mine, and he nodded his head.

I showed up at the appointed time and place, introduced myself to staff at the front desk and was told Michael was on his way. I was ushered down the hall to Rebecca's room, where I stood in the doorway, my flute case slung over my shoulder.

The room was unlike any I had ever seen. Except for a small pathway of vinyl, the entire floor was covered with several four-inch-thick gymnastic style pads, the width of double beds.

There was a dresser drawer along the left wall, on top of a single floor mat. This dresser and the mats were the only furniture. Rebecca sat in a special wheelchair at the end of a vinyl path on my left. The padded back of the chair was several inches higher than the top of her head. The sides of the armrests were also tall, several inches wide, and bent forward like narrow wings to protect her arms. The back of the leg supports were similarly padded. The padding was necessary protection because of her continual random movements. She flayed about with her head, arms, and legs jerking violently. I could not understand anything she said, although I think she was responding to my greeting.

"Hello, I'm RuthiE. I'm here to play native flute for you."

Michael arrived, looked at me, and nodded hello. He looked

to Rebecca, smiled, waved a hand, and lowered himself to the floor, on the mat to the right of the door, leaning his back on the wall, and said, "Go ahead and play." He closed his eyes.

I sat on the mat next to the dresser and pulled a flute from the case. Having never played flute for a patient, much less one with Huntington's, I was tentative. I had no idea what was going to happen. I sat for a moment with my flute, focusing on my breath. I thought of Raven's words, "It is your responsibility to put the heart into the flute."

I took a deep breath and softly exhaled while keeping my eyes on Rebecca. A long low note sounded. I witnessed Rebecca's movements stop. I could hardly believe it!! She was still as a stone except for her right hand which continued to move gently back and forth like a metronome. All movement had stopped. I had been so concerned, not knowing what could happen. An increase in violent movements? A grand mal seizure? I didn't know. I certainly was not expecting no movement. Remembering exactly what Raven had said, "This is a healing instrument."

While I changed flutes, the violent, involuntary movements began again. I had been playing for a half hour when I noticed Michael had shifted his body. He was now flat on his back, one leg straight out, the other bent at the knee. He was fast asleep.

Because Rebecca's response to the flute was so positive, future visits were made without Michael. I played for over an hour until my wood flutes became too moist inside, a condition known as "watering out." I eventually was able to understand her speech. She thanked me with great effort. "Ya-er mus-soc guh-eves-me-com-furt, an ress."

I visited Rebecca one last time before our move to Arizona. I had a nagging feeling I had forgotten something as I drove away. I checked for flutes, purse, water bottle. All were beside me on the car seat. What could I have left behind? I glanced in the rearview mirror and saw the Puyallup SNF disappear. It dawned on me I would not be coming back. I had left behind a big piece of my heart.

DEE

    She "held court" in Room 4 located at the west end of Kanmar Place. The room was a long rectangle barely wide enough for the length of her hospital bed which divided the room evenly in half. The space between the bedroom door and her bed had a nightstand which held her journal and pen. There was a small, round table with two armchairs for visitors. The area on the far side of the bed had a credenza along the wall for a lamp and vase of flowers. On the wall above the credenza hung a 6x3-foot framed poster. It was an image of a winged woman with long brunette hair wearing a navy dress with a billowing skirt. A modern-day angel perhaps? Dee was quite fond of this image with which she conversed. Dee told me her name was DeMaria.

    Dee was one of the happiest hospice patients I have ever met. Each day was new, filled with adventure and gratitude.

Dee quit drinking the morning she discovered her car, parked in the garage, had a broken headlight and crumpled fender on the passenger side. She had absolutely no recall of the night before and wondered how she had gotten home. She waited anxiously for the police who never came. She quit her high-pressure CEO job, which involved heavy drinking after office hours, and joined AA to turn her life around. It was only a short time later she was diagnosed with terminal liver cancer and elected to go on hospice. I learned little else about her personal life.

She quickly became a staff favorite because of her remarkable outlook, living each day to the fullest.

One of the aides said, "Dee told me nobody has ever loved her like we do."

The entire length of the wall at the foot of her bed had windows below the ceiling. They were two-feet-wide and uncovered. The view was the ever-changing light from the sun on treetops, the sky, and clouds.

Dee accepted the flute music I offered. Then, with tears streaming down her face, asked, "Is it in your job description to play flute and make people cry?" Her response to my flute playing is not uncommon. Sometimes a patient or caregiver will touch a hand to their heart, look deeply into my eyes, nod thanks, and not say anything.

I asked, "What came up for you?"

She stared at the ceiling for a moment. Then with a calm expression said. "Your music makes me realize that what is going to happen is going to happen in the way it is supposed to."

This soul connection through the flute was the beginning of our relationship. Dee was not ready to talk about death directly, although she was busy with her funeral plans and taking care of other business.

In an early session, she was writing thank-you notes when I arrived. With a big smile, she exclaimed she was celebrating her friends and her gratitude for them. We discussed songwriting as a way of telling a story or sharing sentiment.

Note cards and envelopes were strewn across the bed, on top of, and around the "over the bed table" she used as a writing desk. She repeated words in a sing-song voice and asked me to play flute to accompany her words. Together we created this song:

You dropped me a line,
I celebrate, I celebrate!

You took the time!
I celebrate, I celebrate!
I'm so grateful for my friends.
Amen.

I offered her the tingshas and showed her how to use them. Tingshas are brass discs 2.5 inches in diameter attached to one another by a leather cord, approximately 15-inches long. It is a lightweight instrument that has a strong chime quality with multiple harmonics. Traditionally used to open or close meditation sessions, I suggested Dee might wish to use them to emphasize her feelings of celebration.

We collaborated on flute tones to fit her words and celebratory mood. At the words, "I celebrate," Dee struck the tingshas together. Tentatively at first, then with more enthusiasm, she swung her arms over her head wildly, causing the chimes to ring out joyfully again and again. She threw back her head and laughed, "This is so much fun!"

We played and sang this song as part of each visit, it always brought forth a smile from both of us. In a later session, Dee was photographed playing the tingshas. She attached the picture on the large poster of DeMaria over her bed. As Dee's life ebbed, she was able to lift the tingshas only a short height, then not at all except in her imagination. At those times, she softly stroked the tingshas and smiled at the photograph.

When I asked Dee if there was anything she needed to do or had left undone, she lamented, "I love poetry, but I've never written a poem." After music and meditation, holding the intention, she wished to create a "present-feeling" poem. Dee randomly selected words from the word bowl of magnetic words. She arranged the words on a small magnetic board and created the following poem.

"You teach them to remember a sweet summer and celebrate. Tell my ears they like eternity."

Dee read the words aloud, smiled, and said, "WOW!" We had spent several sessions reviewing her life; what she had felt good about and things she regretted. This short poem validated her life and her anticipated afterlife.

On several visits ,Dee, asked me to read part of a poem from Rilke's *Book of Hours, Love Poems to God.*

I read, " You said live, out loud, and die, you said lightly, and over and over again you said be. Just be. To make of you a bridge over the chasm of everything."

When I asked Dee, "What resonated with you?"

She said, "Chasm." She then asked me to scribe her response in her journal. The opportunity to speak and have her words read back to her validated her feelings and thoughts.

Over the Chasm---
That's where I'm going,
You help by being here
With your flute,
By being you.

****

Across the chasm
I imagine beauty,
Love, friends,
And Lots of flowers.

***

The closing of the chasm will be
What I have been
Doing here.

***

I prepared all my life
For death.

One doesn't think about that.
At least I never did
Until now.

I was thankful for the education gained in my Expression Arts Therapy program. I recognized that the sounds of the flute helped Dee enter her imagination, allowing her to express herself in different ways. She would often gaze at the poster of DeMaria flying above the credenza, and instead of flying nestled between DeMaria's wings, she would imagine wandering in the forests and glens or swimming with the swans while DeMaria soared overheard and kept loving watch over her. In these explorations, Dee left the reality of the bed in which she lay, dying.

One afternoon, returning from her imagined world, she told me, "I don't need to be afraid of death. DeMaria will be with me."

Another time she tearfully reported, "I can hear her wings. She told me not to be afraid—she would carry me and keep me safe."

About that time, Dee was interviewed by a reporter from the *Arizona Sun* who asked her about hospice and music. She was quoted saying, "I don't hurt when she plays."

Later, she told me how surprised she was to hear herself say that as she claimed she had no pain, except maybe, "Here," touching her head and then her heart. Demonstrating the flute affected Dee physiologically as well as emotionally. As Dee became weaker and entered the pre-active stage of dying, she was still able to express herself through the arts.

When she told me she was "stewing" about things, I suggested she dictate a "*Stew List.*"

She said, "I'm *stewing about loneliness; my friends going out and doing things."*

I asked, "Do you mean without you?"

Dee gasped, "Oh my! I just remembered when I was four years old, I was excluded from a fun event by playmates. I think this is the root of all my present loneliness. I can't believe I've kept that memory buried for 73 years!"

Dee called her inner four-year old "Emily" and asked me to play a "meandering" tune on the G flute. The G key is associated with the throat chakra, center of self-expression.

The tune I played proved to be an opening for self-expression for both of us. I had no idea what I was going to play, but as I imagined a little girl, the words "*hop, skip, jump*" came to mind. Along with these words came a lively, meandering, improvised tune. Dee's eyes closed, and a slight smile softened her face. I noticed Dee's feet move ever-so-slightly beneath the covers. When I put the flute down, Dee's eyes flew open, and she excitedly reported, "Oh RuthiE, I'm not lonely anymore! I was twirling and dancing with a new set of friends. They taught me to hop, skip, and jump!"

We laughed when I said, "Those are the exact words I was thinking while I played! Did you read my mind?"

The staff became so attached to Dee that they could not handle it when she became comatose. Often the staff could be found crying at Dee's bedside or in the laundry room, or worse, ignoring other patients. It was difficult for them to maintain their professional distance. She was quickly transferred to the In-Patient Unit where her breathing became so shallow, the rise and fall of her chest were barely discernible. Her position and stillness reminded me of the catafalques of saints I had seen in European cathedrals. I sat next to her bed in silence and imagined she was already gone. Dee said on one of the last visits, when she was still verbal, "The air feels soft." She died peacefully several days later.

I wrote the following poem, reflecting on our time together.

Imagining Dee with DeMaria

The air feels soft on her face
Nestled there between the wings of DeMaria
Who holds the world gently in her outstretched hands.
A dove escort and a rainbow,
Swans swimming below in the enchanted land
Are her view.
She floats on the air high above the Earth
On the back of DeMaria,
Universe Angel.
The air is soft on her face
As they travel together on this journey
Exploring the mysteries of life
And life after life
Her fairy angels dance and sing
She is unafraid.
She is unafraid.

NANCY

I am always touched by a dying patient; some touch more deeply than others. Nancy died last night. I sit in her memory today with a heavy heart. She sparkled with childlike joy upon being admitted. Her smile and enthusiasm were infectious until she eventually became bedbound. She loved sunlight until eventually, it began to hurt her eyes, and she asked for the heavy drapes to be closed like a shroud.

Nancy had laid on her back with both arms stretched out in front and above her. She moved them in wide circles and figure 8's while I played flute in the dim light.

Her daughter, Suzanne, once asked, "Mom, what are you doing?"

"I'm painting all these gorgeous colors I see."

After a few moments, she turned onto her right side and reached out to touch something I could not see. A bit of her sparkle returned as she said clearly, "I love angels. It's happening so fast, you know, like warp speed."

I did not stop playing to respond.

I had been assigned to meet Nancy and her family on Veterans Day at 2 p.m. Nancy had been so vibrant; now, two weeks later, she was bed-bound and barely responsive. Her family came from out-of-state to sign her onto hospice.

When I arrived at The Fountains, Nancy's senior living community, the lobby was filled with rows of folding chairs facing a two-foot-high stage platform decorated with a drape of red, white, and blue bunting across the front. There was a large American flag on a stand next to a microphone on the stage. A heavyset woman with fluffy white hair, wearing a powder blue suit, was standing at the microphone. Her elderly audience with canes and walkers testified to disabilities as well as age. When their applause died down, the woman at the mic smiled, nodded, and began to sing "God Bless America." Her voice was a clear soprano with a slight warble befitting her generation. She reminded me of Barbara Bush. I had never heard Mrs. Bush sing, but I doubt it could be lovelier than this woman who looked just like her, including the string of white pearls.

I looked around for Nancy's son-in-law, Tom, who had answered the phone when I called to confirm my appointment. He'd said, "There is a program this afternoon. I'll meet you in the lobby."

I had given Tom my description. "I'm wearing a knee-length, white lab coat. My name and the company logo are embroidered on the upper right chest. I have on a yellow lanyard with my name." Practically every woman and most of the men were wearing white. The yellow lanyard was distinctive enough for Tom to find me.

"Are you from hospice?"

"Yes. I'm RuthiE," I shook his outstretched hand.

"I'm Tom, and this is my daughter, Holly." He nodded toward a beautiful young girl, about 10 years old, with shoulder-length, reddish blonde hair. She was holding onto her father's left hand with both of her own.

Tom motioned for me to follow him. Once in the empty hallway on the other side of the crowd, Holly ran ahead and disappeared around a corner at the end of the long hallway. She was waiting for us at a bank of four elevators and pushed the "up" button to the third floor.

"It's easier to guide someone than try to give directions," Tom explained as I followed him with Holly at his side. We went down one long hallway after another, turning left, then right, and left again before arriving at a door marked with a large name sign *"Nannette and Milton."*

Tom opened the door without knocking and gestured for me to enter. He slipped behind me with Holly and went to the back of the room where an elderly man sat on a high-back wing chair.

Three women on my right immediately jumped to their feet. A fourth woman to my left remained seated in an overstuffed chair, her swollen feet propped on an ottoman, fuzzy pink slippers matched the pink turban on her head.

I was taken aback as I looked at the assembly. It felt like I was standing up close and in front of a small stage. The women established their role with rapid fire introductions.

"Hi, I'm Sally Lorraine, oldest daughter, Tom's wife. She was tall and slim with short, brown hair, and a no-nonsense manner.

"Hi, I'm Suzanne, youngest daughter." Sally's look-alike with long hair. Her voice was soft, as Sally's was firm.

From the corner in the back of the room, "I'm Milt, the husband." He only offered a slight wave of his hand and did not stand. He reminded me of an owl on a perch with his black, horn-rimmed glasses. Tom and Holly sat next to him. A young woman with soft features and blonde hair in a pageboy stood next to the woman seated on the overstuffed chair with her feet on the ottoman. "Hi, I'm Maggie, Gram's oldest granddaughter and Holly's sister." She sat down on the arm of the overstuffed chair.

Expectant eyes were now on me. "Hi, I'm RuthiE, the nurse." I looked to the thin, pale woman on my left. She held her hands out in front of her, palms up. Her smile became broader as she said brightly, "I guess that makes me Nancy, the patient!"

There seemed to be a light emanating from her countenance, her face smooth and peaceful. I felt compelled to put my hands together in prayer position, the way yogis do, with a slight nod of my head. "Namaste," I said.

A flash of puzzlement crossed Nancy's face at first. I realized she might not understand the meaning of my gesture and the unfamiliar word.

"The Light in me honors the light in you," I translated.

She sat up straighter and exclaimed, "Oh, I love it!"

Then she put her hands in prayer position in front of her heart and reverently returned my greeting, "Namaste."

I loved her immediately from this moment of connection. I listened, enraptured, while she spoke.

"I have cancer of everything. I forget the original site—breast maybe," she said, looking at Sally.

The oldest daughter clarified, "It's spread to her liver, brain, lungs, and bone."

Suzanne interjected, "She just finished a second round of chemo. She saw her doctor Friday. He suggested hospice."

Sally added, "As a matter of fact, her doctor's partner suggested hospice three months ago."

Maggie spoke up, "I know the doctor suggested hospice, but Grandma is slated for a new trial of drugs in 12 weeks."

There is a doctor in town whose reputation was that when he says, "Time for hospice," the patient had little time left. It could be less than a week; perhaps, maybe only a day or two, even when the patient is scheduled for more treatment.

Nancy's oncologist was that doctor. I explained that hospice is a Medicare benefit, and that Nancy would be assigned a team. A registered nurse case manager would visit and together, they would decide how often the RN would visit and how frequently the home health aide would come. The primary caregiver would have responsibility for organizing the patient's care.

Nancy listened to my explanation of hospice philosophy, supporting the patient and family, making each day count until she dies. She nodded her head, then said, "I just want to get stronger."

I sat on the ottoman sharing space with the pink fuzzy slippers. I looked directly into her eyes and gently, but firmly, said, "Nancy, getting stronger isn't going to happen; you will be loved and taken care of. You will not get stronger."

Having met each of the family members and completed the required assessment protocol required by Medicare, I asked, "Are there any questions?"

Maggie had been standing close, leaning over Nancy, her left arm around her grandmother's shoulder and her right hand resting on the chair arm for balance. Tears welled up and spilled out of her eyes at my words. She stood abruptly and walked rapidly into the adjacent bedroom.

I followed her.

She was sitting next to her mother on the edge of a twin bed wiping her eyes with a tissue. I sat on the opposite twin bed and waited for her to look at me.

"I'm sorry for being so direct."

Maggie blew her nose. "It's okay, I knew this. I just didn't want to hear it."

I took a deep breath. Intuitively, I knew Nancy would not be alive in 12 weeks, but I did not want to dash any hope her granddaughter had.

"Maggie, it is okay for your grandmother to go on hospice today, and if she wants to go on the drug trial in 12 weeks, she can sign off hospice."

Maggie nodded and smiled, gave her grandmother a gentle hug, and a big smile when we both returned to the living room.

Nancy said, "Good, here you are. I thought I would have to come get you."

I discussed Nancy's need to have assistance with daily care, and she could not be left alone. Sally said she and Tom could help until they returned to California in two days. Maggie said she could help on weekends—she was a full-time freshman at the University of Arizona. Suzanne was a freelance artist and could arrange to extend her leave of absence. Milt, who said he was the primary caregiver, quickly revealed he had no concept of this responsibility.

When I asked, "Do you cook?"

Milt said, "No, I don't. Never have. I go to the dining room. That's why we moved here."

Noticing food stains on the front of his shirt, I asked, "What about laundry?"

"Oh, Nancy does it all. I don't even know where the laundry room is."

"Nancy will need help to the toilet and shower," I said.

"I can't do that," Milt responded. "She has always done that herself. I don't see so well, and I'm unsteady on my feet."

The family exchanged looks as Milt answered my questions. It was apparent he could not take care of himself, much less Nancy. I said, "It's okay, Milt. I will have the on-call social worker come today. She will help sort out a plan for Nancy's care and safety."

I believe eyes are the windows to the soul. Nancy's soul spoke volumes. Her smile was brilliant. While she was articulate and voiced her thoughts, she just couldn't seem to get over the fact I had come to see her on Veteran's Day holiday. While I was explaining the election of the Medicare benefit and operation of her care team, she turned to Sally, smiling, with a look of joy.

She finally pointed at me and said, "Isn't she just something, Sally? I'd like to take her home with me!" She did not seem to remember I was in her new home. We exchanged "Namastes," then I said goodbye.

The following week, I was surprised and happy to see Nancy at Kanmar Place. Kanmar is a five-bed, private-pay-assisted, living facility created by Casa Hospice. I play Native American flute for the residents who live there on Tuesdays and Thursdays. I did not know Nancy's family transferred Milt to The Fountains Assisted Living and moved Nancy into Kanmar for end-of-life care. When I saw her, I was not sure she would recognize me.

Her smile lightened. Her face clearly said, "Yes, of course, I remember you!" She was sitting in a winged-back chair next to a large window overlooking a private garden patio filled with large plants and vines. She opened her arms to me and said, "WOW!"

Nancy responded as if I was the most wonderful person she'd ever met.

"How could I forget you! How did you ever FIND me?"

I believe in recognizing Divine Guidance. I was meant to be there with Nancy at the end of her life.

Suzanne had extended her temporary leave-of-absence and was there too.

She said, "I am so glad you will play flute for Mom. Do you mind if I drum and chant while you play? I practice a 'Lakota-based faith.'"

"Mind? Of could not! What a wonderful way to pray." The three of us sat together in silence except for my flute, the soft rhythms of the drum and Suzanne's voice.

Nancy joined in with her smile and arm gestures. "Painting beautiful colors," she said.

I was sitting at the head of Nancy's bed one morning when Sally visited during "Lakota Prayer." I stepped into the hall to give her privacy as she leaned over to whisper her love and farewell. I could feel tears filling my eyes.

When I entered Nancy's room several days later, her eyes held an anxious expression, as if to say, *"What the heck is happening to me?"*

I reassured her softly. "Everything is okay, Nancy."

I began to play softly as her expression softened and relaxed. She closed her eyes just as Suzanne came in. Instead of picking up the drum as she usually did, she leaned over Nancy's bed and spoke softly to her mother. I was sitting in my usual spot by the door and could see their silhouetted profiles. A radiance of love traveled back and forth between them, little motions, soft words, smiles, a kiss, a touch. It was so moving. My tears began to flow, but I kept on playing. Suzanne moved to her usual place at the foot of the bed and began to drum. We had found a musical connection between us—beginning and ending in unison strictly guided by intuition.

The heavy drapes were held together with a clip in the center of two halves that did not quite meet, leaving a V-shaped opening at the top. Sunlight was hitting the ceiling, leaving the rest of the room dimly lit. The room was silent when our prayer song came to its natural end.

Meeting Nancy had such an effect on me. She was just so alive. She looked at me with such unconditional love and light. Nancy slowly opened her eyes and smiled into the sunshine on the ceiling. She clearly said, "Raccoon."

I was puzzled.

Suzanne looked at me when I asked, "What did she say?"

"Raccoon. She said, 'Raccoon.' I'm sure of it."

Suzanne smiled and said, "I've been wondering how Mom would come to me from the Spirit world. She just told me."

Suzanne invited me to play flute at the small, private memorial while she walked among the guests, drumming and chanting

Lakota prayers. She concluded the ceremony telling the guests assembled about her mother's last word, `raccoon' which is how she said she would contact me from the Spirit world. Suzanne went on to tell everyone that on her way to the service, she had seen a most unusual sight on the freeway median–a mother raccoon and two babies. That means that she is with us today.

BETH

I saw Beth three times at two-week intervals for one-and-a-half-hour visits, before she died. At the request of her family, I participated in her memorial Catholic Mass.

Beth reminded me of a loving, benevolent queen as she lay on her wide hospital-style bed on top of a feather bed comforter, surrounded by many fluffed pillows, with the head of the bed elevated. All the bedding was white with gold trim to match her pajamas. Her smile and gestures were welcoming and sincere. She began to tell me of her "adventures" she'd had throughout her life and was quite open in speaking of life coming to an end. Her speech clear, definite, and full of expression, as she said, "Your visits are to help me on my journey."

I bring flutes of different keys to allow patients a choice. Beth chose a key of E. It is believed the E flute relates to the 3rd chakra or energy center located above the navel in the solar plexus. It is associated with the color yellow, vitality, energy, and intellect.

Native Flute music is the gateway to our communication and connection. I played the E flute at my first visit with Beth. She wanted to join in and shook a gourd rattle. Her granddaughter, Nellie, held the heartbeat on my handmade rawhide drum. Two other family members, her brother, Ted, and granddaughter, Elayne, joined in with egg shakers and tingshas. My instructions from those who taught me were, *"listen to my music, and your heart's music is how we play together."* With that in mind, we improvised together for 10 minutes or more, the song coming to its own natural conclusion. We sat in silence for another minute or two, breathing in the peace and sacredness of our shared experience. The calm, gentle energy was palpable. It reminded me of being in church.

Two weeks later, on the following visit, Beth's granddaughters, Nellie and Elayne, were present. They explained they were taking a break from college to be Beth's primary caregivers during the day. Their mother, Martha, worked full-time as an administrative assistant to a high school principal. She could not afford to take time off.

Again, I played the key of E with my native flute. Nellie, Elayne, and Beth sang *"Going Home,"* an old hymn Beth remembered from her youth. Then, at Beth's request, we sang a newer Catholic hymn, *"On Eagles Wings,"* a favorite that had been sung at her grandson, Jake's, funeral. The chorus is especially powerful.

And He will raise you up on eagles' wings,
Bear you on the breath of dawn,
Make you to shine like the sun,
And hold you in the palm of His hand.

Singing helped Beth tearfully share her sorrow about Jake's death. He was killed in a motorcycle accident three years ago when he was eighteen. Her tears and talking about the accident alleviated some emotional pain she held since his death.

When I arrived two weeks later, Beth was upset. "I'm still here! What's taking so long? This is happening too slowly!"

I let her talk without interruption. "I'm ready ... I've said everything I've needed to say." After a few moments of silence, she added, "except write my own obituary. I waited too long to do that. Now, I'm too weak to hold a pencil."

I asked if she might dictate the information to Nellie who agreed to be the scribe. Beth said, "Maybe. Please play your flute." She closed her eyes, and at the first tones, she smiled, threw up her hands, and declared, "I'm gone, I'm soaring!"

When Beth opened her eyes, she said, "OK, I'm ready to begin."

I wasn't sure what she meant. We had just discussed her "getting on with dying," but she explained she was ready to dictate her obituary. Nellie settled into a dining room chair next to the head of Beth's bed with a yellow legal size note pad and wrote her grandmother's words.

Beth mentioned all who had come before her, beginning with a "great-great" ancestor who served in the Confederate Army, "in the war between the States." She went down through her entire lineage, and I was briefly reminded of scripture and those verses on generations who were "begat" and begotten.

When she got to the present generation of who she would leave behind, she said she was too tired to go on naming names. Nellie said she would ask her mother to help finish the litany which would become Beth's legacy. Beth's obituary was printed in the Arizona Daily Star as she dictated—unedited and unfinished. It filled half a column. I regret I did not keep a copy because it was more of a genealogy report than an individual's obituary.

Beth, a devout practicing Catholic, still had questions about the afterlife. I didn't have the answer, but I taught her a "Spirit" song from the weekend intensive when I was studying music for my Master of Arts in Expressive Arts Therapy. Beth, Nellie, and Elayne found it very affirming and memorized it.

Spirit am I
Blessed am I
I am the infinite within my Soul
I have no beginning and
I have no end
All this I am.

Beth then wondered, "What will become of me, after I die?" Thinking of our visits, I said, "I believe you will be an angel."

She replied, "I'd rather be an eagle!"

While I played flute, Beth appeared to be in deep meditation until she opened her eyes and smiled. "I am sprouting my eagle feathers."

She closed her eyes. We watched as her respirations became

deep and even again. She was sleeping soundly when I left. I believe she was *flying* in her imaginary realm. Beth died peacefully several days later.

Nellie delivered the eulogy at Beth's memorial Mass. She concluded by saying, "Mom's work schedule kept her away during RuthiE's visits which Grandma loved so much." Nellie paused, looked directly at her mother, Martha, sitting alone in the front pew, and took a deep breath. "Mother, now it's your time to experience Grandmother's time with RuthiE."

This was my cue to stand and play flute while Nellie played drum and Elayne shook the gourd rattle Beth had held during our jam sessions. In unison, they softly whispered the *Spirit* song we sang with Beth every visit.

Spirit am I
Blessed am I
I am the infinite within my soul
I have no beginning and
I have no end
All this I am

This was the first time I met Martha. She began to laugh, and then she cried. She hugged me over and over again. She thanked me and heartily thanked her daughters for recreating the energy we had all shared with her mother. She said, "I felt so guilty I couldn't be home with my mother. My girls told me how special your visits were. Thank you for sharing that experience with me today. It was like being there with you and Mom."

LEYA

"Hello, Casa de la Luz? This is Lisa M. I'm calling from Utah. I have researched hospices in the Tucson area. I've selected Casa because you have a native flute player on staff. It's mentioned on your website. My mom, Leya, has terminal cancer. She's Lakota Sioux, and I want the flute player to visit her."

The RN case manager made the referral for me to visit and offered native flute as part of Leya's care plan. The paperwork stated:

> "Intervention/frequency: visit one time a week to provide NAF music and drumming with opportunity for patient to engage in storytelling and life review."

Leya asked me to play "Amazing Grace" at every visit. Every

time I finished playing, she would say, "Play it again." Sometimes she would invite visitors to come listen or sing. "It's a beautiful song to sing along." And because she loved it so, she said, "Play it again."

If her eyes were closed, she always opened them slightly at the first notes, as if opening her eyes would help her hear better. I began to improvise alternate endings to keep the song fresh and alive.

Every visit followed a ritual pattern of greetings—her offer of coffee which I always politely declined, a bit of reminiscing, and discovery over time of how similar our lives had been. We made our own clothes out of flour sack prints, lived in houses heated by wood-burning stoves, and we heated water for bathing. Leya appreciated our similarities miles and years apart. We shared "little bits" of personal history—her mother, grandmother, powwows, and her longing to hear "the old women singing."

She once said to me, "Your every wish is my command." I think what she really meant was her every wish was *my* command. In response to her longing to hear the "old women singing at powwow," I went online to a native flute community. I was able to procure cassette tapes of Lakota women singing. Leya cried "happy tears" as she listened and sang along in Lakota.

Slowly, over time, I learned Leya and her husband, Wes', story …

"I was a social worker. My husband was an alcoholic and left me with five kids; six, really, but my eleven-year-old son, Jason, was killed by a drunk driver when he was riding his bike home from school."

Nodding her head toward Wes, Leya's voice was soft and matter-of-fact as she concluded, "That's how we met." As dainty and frail as she was, she seemed even more so next to Wes' 6'4" frame. He was a brick of a man with a military buzz haircut and tired eyes. He was a retired motorcycle highway patrolman who led the funeral procession that took Leya's son's body to the cemetery.

"Friends introduced us." After Wes' wife died, we decided to get married. I had five kids, and he had three, and then we were expecting our own baby. But we couldn't handle it," she said sadly.

Wes interrupted by stating firmly. "And the Brady Bunch we were not! The kids could not, would not, get along. We knew it wasn't going to work. We got a divorce and an abortion. We stayed in touch, and when the youngest, the two-year-old, turned 18, we got back together and came to Tucson."

I don't know how long they had been apart, back together, or had been in Tucson. I do know that they lived in a large trailer community comprised of permanent single- and double-wide units. Theirs was a two bedroom, two bathroom, fully furnished double-wide. After Leya came on hospice, a hospital bed was set up in the open living/dining area so Leya could be included in all activities.

Three of Leya's children, Lisa, Danni, and J.R., visited several times, traveling by Greyhound bus. Leya was especially thrilled when Wes found her stash of beads and gave them to J.R. who did beading work that Leya had taught him.

Leya had been a smoker in the past. When she was told she could do whatever she wanted because of her terminal diagnosis, she decided to take up smoking again. She would occasionally ask for a cigarette, and after a few puffs, let it burn out in the ashtray.

One day, after I played the "E" flute, she said, "I want to smoke."

Leya had never said this before. I gave her a lit cigarette

which she held between her thumb and index finger. She drew smoke into her mouth and blew it out in a slow deliberate manner several times before discarding the cigarette in the ash tray.

She turned to me and asked, "May I play *Grandmother?*"

Grandmother is the name of my "E" flute which is made of lightning-struck poplar. I handed it to Leya. She held it with her palms underneath while I supported the end. She made no attempt to cover the holes. She held the flute's mouthpiece to her lips and whispered into it. I closed my eyes and listened to the soft cooing sounds.

I said to Leya, "I hear mourning doves."

She smiled, closed her eyes, and continued to play the soft sounds and whispered, "an Indian song."

Leya then blew gently several times into the flute mouthpiece in the same repetitive manner as she had drawn in and blown out cigarette smoke. She then handed the flute back to me. I was reminded of a pipe ceremony and how the Native Americans view tobacco as sacred. Her choice of words, her tender reverent manner holding the flute, prompted me to say, "Leya, that reminded me of a pipe ceremony."

She smiled and said, "Yes, the pipe."

The following week, while playing flute, I distinctly heard a songbird, although I was not sure if it was outside the window or from a clock in another room. Leya heard it too and asked, "Where is the cow?"

"There is no cow. It is a bird," I said.

She said, "That is what I meant."

A short time later, she asked, "Did you see the young boy leave the room?" She was looking to the left where a hall led between the living room and the end of the trailer.

"No, Leya, I didn't see anyone."

She looked puzzled, saying, "Well, he just left."

I have heard of people who are dying seeing things that others cannot. "It sounds like you are seeing energy forms that I can't."

Leya smiled and made direct eye contact with me. "Yes, I'm more complete."

She continued to talk. Her speech was clear, but very soft, at times whispering as though she was speaking to someone who I could not see. I was unable to follow the conversation.

With no more to contribute to the conversation, I thought aloud, "You might be between worlds."

She smiled and replied, "Yes, I am betwixt and between."

She continued to smile and nod while I continued to play flute. When her home health aide arrived to bathe her, I said goodbye. Leya reached up, put her arm around my neck, and said, "I'm going to miss you. Goodbye, sweet girl."

One Tuesday morning, I came as usual and found Leya in bed instead of the recliner chair.

Wes said, "She requested medication for pain, so she might be cloudy."

Leya was not cloudy. However, I thought she looked forlorn. "You look sad."

She nodded, "Yes, I'm glad you came. I have no one to talk to. I just found out how sick I am. I have to make plans."

"What kind of plans, Leya?"

"Well, for one, I want you to play "Amazing Grace" at my funeral. And I want the name and phone number of a medicine man. I need to talk to one."

Wes was sitting at the dining table, his eyes full of tears. He stood up and said,

"I can't deal with all this funeral talk." He blew his nose into a handkerchief from the back pocket of his jeans and slipped out the side door.

Leya's eyes followed him.

"We are going to renew our wedding vows so we have a better way of talking to each other," she said.

"Can you come next Wednesday instead of Tuesday? I want you to play 'Amazing Grace' at the ceremony."

I spoke to Jan, Leya's team chaplain who is an ordained interfaith minister. I shared with her Leya's desire to speak to a medicine man and to renew her marriage vows in a church. I smiled thinking about her initial statement, "My every wish was her command." Actually, it turned out to be the opposite.

It was a lovely ceremony and celebration. Casa staff turned the screened patio into a chapel with crepe paper draped around from the ceiling, and bouquets of flowers, and even a wedding cake had been provided. Leya wore a new pink pantsuit which her daughter, Danni, purchased. Leya sat in a new wheelchair brought to the front through an aisle that divided the hospice team and Leya's children. Wes was waiting for her at the "altar." He wore a new white shirt with a white rose boutonniere and a very big smile.

The entire care team was present: RN case manager, chaplain, social worker, bath aide, and the volunteer who did the decorations. There were six of us, no small feat to coordinate our schedules to help one patient and her family celebrate this special day. I don't know how many times I played "Amazing Grace" which was also sung several times in unison.

Leya's body had been prepared for viewing at home as is often the case when cremation is planned. During our visits, she had always opened her eyes when I played "Amazing Grace." As I began to play her favorite song, I actually thought I saw her eyes open slightly. I dismissed this as wishful thinking.

When I finished, I stepped back from the bed. Leya's daughter, Lisa, stepped forward.

She gently closed Leya's eyelids. "I thought I saw her eyes open," she said.

Having heard Leya and Wes' story gave me a larger understanding of her love for this song after all they had shared, suffered, and endured. To be together again at the end of Leya's life was truly, grace. Just amazing.

GONZALES

"They asked for you...by name!" said the call coordinator.

"But I don't know a patient named Gonzales." Truth is, I was on my way to visit patients on the east side. I did not want to be diverted to the south end of town to pronounce the death of someone I couldn't even remember. Especially, with another on-call RN already in that neck of the woods. Arizona state law permits an RN to pronounce a death which means the nurse testifies and fills out the documents for the physician who will sign the death certificate.

The call coordinator insisted, "They must know you from somewhere ..."

I racked my brain on the 40-minute drive to the south side of town to pronounce the death of a "Mr. Gonzales," wondering why did they ask for me? I rolled the patient's name over my tongue and the address through my mind. Neither rang a bell. It is true, sometimes I see many patients one time only, and then not again until death. Maybe I visited after hours to help with a crisis. Perhaps that's how Mr. Gonzales knew me.

As soon as I drove up the long gravel driveway with a barbed wire fence, I was certain I had never been there. The houses were separated by a bleak desert landscape, scattered with miles of cacti. As I pulled in, a young man directed me through the narrow driveway alongside the clapboard house. I pulled up in the back and parked by a separate dilapidated building badly in need of paint.

As I got out of the car with my stethoscope and clipboard, a young, dark-haired woman came out of the back door, rushing toward me. She called out frantically, "Did you bring your flute?"

Well, that's different. No hello. No thanks for coming. No, are you the hospice nurse? But, did I bring my flute? How does she know I play flute?

She saw that I was confused and did the best she could to answer the questions that were swirling around in my brain.

"I want you to play flute for my dad," she said. "It's on the website."

A look of relief washed across her face when I said, "Yes, I brought my flute."

"Where is it?" she asked, her eyes searching me for proof that what I said was true.

I turned to my car and opened the door. Behind the passenger seat was a small flute made of oak which could not be damaged by the fiery Arizona heat. With my back to her, I wondered what would have happened if I didn't have the flute with me.

The woman finally introduced herself as I showed her the flute. "I'm Silvia. It's my father who died. I want you to play flute for him."

Dutifully, I followed her up the steps and entered the small, cluttered kitchen through the back door.

Silvia stopped when she saw her mother, Maria, who was small, shorter than five feet, and sturdily built. She wore a brightly colored apron over a faded housedress. "Mom, this is the hospice nurse."

Looking toward me, she said, "This is my mom, Maria."

"Hello, I am sorry for your loss," I said, still not understanding how I got there.

Maria's voice was soft, and she did not make eye contact

when she lowered her eyes and said, "Gracias." I watched her use the corner of her apron to wipe a tear that escaped beneath the frame of her glasses.

Maria said something in Spanish to Silvia and the young boy whom I hadn't noticed sitting at the table with a plate of scrambled eggs. Silvia nodded, and the boy stood and followed Maria from the room with his breakfast. They both disappeared into the shadows of the living room.

Silvia gestured for me to approach the table. "If you need a place to write," she said.

Puzzled, I looked at her. There was nothing to write until after I pronounced her father's death, which reminded me. I hadn't seen him yet. I asked, "Your father is …?"

She turned and opened a door off the kitchen, "In here."

I followed her into a dimly lit, overcrowded bedroom. Along the wall to my left, there was a tall dresser and a wingback chair. Along the right wall was another tall dresser with barely enough room between the foot of the bed and the dresser for a person to pass. On the double bed lay the still body of Mr. Gonzales.

Two overstuffed chairs, smaller than the wingback, a metal folding chair with a cushion, and an ottoman completely filled the space on the far side of the bed. In spite of the crowding, a floor lamp with clothes hooks covered with clothing overflowed next to the head of the bed. A large cross, sans corpus, hung on the wall behind the dead man's head next to the window, which was straight ahead of me. A blackout shade darkened the room.

The room where Mr. Jose Gonzales lived and died had a musty, closed-up smell. The room was so dim, I was concerned I might trip or stub my toe as I approached the bed. When I am called to a death, I am cognizant of the fact this person was alive a short time before my arrival. The family members present have lost someone they love. I take a few moments to reflect on this fact. As I place the stethoscope on the patient's chest and the earpieces into my ears, I explain, "This might look like a strange thing to do, but I am required to listen for heart and breath sounds."

I hesitated to ask Silvia but had to. "Could you please raise the shade and open the window?"

She responded, "My dad liked the room dark. He was always cold."

Although she was conflicted by my request, she raised the black shade allowing brilliant sunlight to stream through the window. Silvia examined the old-fashioned double-paned window, released the latch between top and bottom, and struggled to separate them. They would not budge.

She said what I was thinking. "The light won't bother him now."

After several futile attempts to get some air into the room, she gave up. "Won't open, painted shut."

The unpleasant odor of an unwashed body beginning to decay became stronger. The room was heating up from the sun. I had already listened for heart and lung sounds of which there weren't any. Sitting on the wingback chair with my clipboard making a note of the time and date, I asked, "Do you want me to play flute now?"

"No, not yet," Silvia said.

There are procedures to follow. In addition to recording the time and date of death, the patient's doctor must be notified, the funeral home is called to remove the body, and the pharmacy is asked to remove the patient's name from the computer, so no more refills will be filled. Finally, the hospice office is called so the call coordinator can let the patient services supervisor know and inform the patient's team of the death.

When I explained to Silvia about the necessary phone calls I would be making, I assured her the family would have as much time as they needed to pay respects and to say goodbye before the body was removed from the house. As I spoke, I noticed Mr.

Gonzales' face was visibly dirty. Saliva and mucus had drained from one side of his mouth, and there was dried "sleep" in the inner corner of both of his eyes.

"Silvia, could you bring me a pan of soap and water so we could wash your father's face?"

She jumped at the idea. "Could we give him a bath?"

She seemed eager to explain. "The home health aide came yesterday, and Dad refused. She came back today, and Mom didn't want him disturbed because he was in a coma. He could get really cranky, and since he was not responding, Mom thought it best to leave him alone." She spoke so tenderly looking at her father with such love. I felt moved to ask, "Would you like to help me?"

She looked at me with tears in her eyes, "Yes."

In addition to these procedures, phone calls, and paperwork, a nurse is also tasked with making sure the body is clean and dry for transport to the funeral home. At the moment of death, there is total muscle relaxation which results in soiling. Although the body might be prepared for burial with embalming and dressing at the funeral home or prepared for cremation, I offer the family the opportunity to assist in the caretaking of the deceased if that is their wish.

"Do you have a funeral home?" I asked Silvia. I put my clipboard down and pulled scissors from my scrub coat pocket. Silvia watched as I explained the next procedure. "I will cut off this part of the Foley catheter, water from the balloon inside will drain out, and I will be able to remove the cath."

She stood bewildered as she watched me proceed with agility.

I moved the bedding just enough to expose the double lumen, placed a plastic-backed "Chux" to catch the water and protect the bottom sheet, and snipped off the end of the opening as I spoke. The Foley catheter slipped out with a slight tug, and I wrapped the Chux around it. I gathered up the drainage tubing and collection bag and asked, "Is there a plastic bag or waste basket?"

Silvia held out an oval-shaped metal waste can that was lined with a recycled grocery bag. "He is going to be cremated," she said and handed me the name and phone number of the mortuary. She silently left the room while I called the funeral home to assure them they would be informed when Mr. Gonzales was ready.

Silvia returned moments later with a plastic basin filled with warm soapy water, a couple of washcloths and several folded towels. She was accompanied by two women who took one look at the body on the bed and immediately fled. Silvia and I got to work sponging and drying her father's body. The bed was low to the floor, and we knelt at the side of it to work. I noticed his nails were long and soiled.

"Do you have any clippers?" I asked.

She returned with a small manicure set in a zippered case. "It's mine," she said proudly. "Dad didn't like anyone touching his hands."

Despite what she had just revealed, all ten nails were clipped, filed, and scrubbed. We used a wet cloth to smooth his hair which Silvia brushed and combed, getting the hair part on the left side as she remembered her dad wore it when he was well enough to comb his own hair. We moved down his body and washed, dried, and applied lotion which helped to minimize the odor. Silvia found stick deodorant which we applied under his arms.

One of the women who had come in and turned around returned with a small oscillating fan she put on top of the dresser at the foot of the bed.

I asked Silvia, "Would you like to change the bedding?" Asking about this rather than demanding a linen change allows the family some control. Silvia left the room and returned a moment later. She shook her head, "Mom said we don't have clean sheets."

Silvia took the pillow and turned it over to find to her delight that the underside was unstained. She smiled.

I handed her a clean towel which she used to cover the spill on the sheet next to the pillow. We folded the top sheet down to cover the spill at the top hemline. Silvia pulled a handmade quilt off the back of a chair and placed it over the sheet.

A dead body is difficult to move. We discovered this when we tried to remove Mr. Gonzales' soiled T-shirt and put on one of his plethora of white cotton T-shirts.

I asked Silvia, "May I cut up the back of one of the shirts? Then, all we'll need to do is put the neck part over his head and slip the arms in like putting on a hospital gown."

"I'm sure Mom won't mind," she said.

Her father's face had at least several weeks of whiskers that formed a short and scraggly beard. We both looked at it.

Silvia was no longer shy. "Mom hates it," she said. "Dad was letting it grow. It won't be disrespectful to shave it off, will it?"

I smiled at Silvia's concern and indecision. "Silvia, I have an elderly aunt who is like a mother to me. She always said the body belongs to the bereaved."

Confused, she asked, "What's that supposed to mean?"

"It means your dad is gone and left his body behind, and you may decide what to do with it." Although Silvia was initially confused, within seconds, she instantly understood. "I'll get the razor," she said as she dashed out of the room.

Together, Silvia and I lathered, shaved, and took turns changing blades as needed.

I felt the need to assure her, "Don't worry about nicks or cuts. The blood isn't circulating."

Silvia said, "I was wondering about that, thanks."

By the time we finished, Mr. Gonzales looked like a new man. He was no longer the disheveled man he was when I arrived. He looked *beautiful*. Not forgetting why I was called there, I asked, "Shall I play flute now?"

"In a minute," Silvia said as she left the room.

I stepped outside and called the on-call coordinator to report on my status. "Still here. Might be a little longer."

The call coordinator said, "Did you ever find out why they asked for you?"

"Because I play flute," I responded.

"Well, did you play? You're needed somewhere else."

"Not yet," I said.

Back inside the house, I stood by the door as person after person entered the small room, quietly finding a place to sit or stand. There were low sounds; sniffles and noses being blown. All the chairs and the arms of chairs were filled. People sat on the floor and stood next to the wall between those sitting. It was an endless stream of mourners. I counted silently. It was 25 before I closed my eyes and pressed my back into the door frame to make room for others.

When I opened my eyes, Silvia caught my eye and nodded, "Now, you can play."

The flute I travel with is small. The lowest note it can play is an "A" above the middle C. And, it plays a pentatonic scale to the octave A. It is definitely not my flute of choice to play in a circumstance such as this. I would prefer something with a lower, more somber tone.

I closed my eyes and said a silent prayer. Lifting the flute to my lips, I blew softly. The first couple of notes were a melancholy sound in a minor key. I have no idea what followed over the next two or three minutes. When I lowered the flute, there was silence. Bowed heads, tears, and people smiling, despite their tears, surrounded me.

The woman who had squeezed into the space immediately to my left turned to me with eyes filled with tears. "That was so beautiful. What was it?"

Uncertain if she was asking about the instrument or the name of the song, I did not answer, holding onto the sacredness of the moment.

The answer was that it was a melody that had been channeled through me.

The awed women stood, patiently awaiting my response.

Finally, I said, "Grace."

Another woman wiped a tear and said, "Amazing."

Yes, I agreed. Amazing grace.

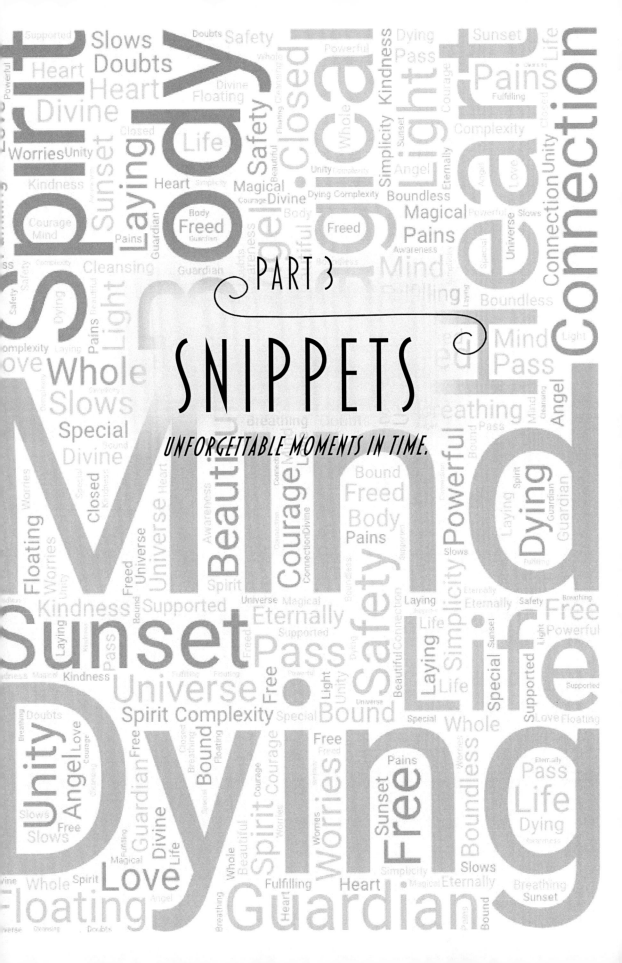

PART 3
SNIPPETS
UNFORGETTABLE MOMENTS IN TIME.

STEVE

The case manager said, "He has a flute. His wife said he wants to learn to play. Will you please teach him?"

What she didn't tell me was that Steve had chronic obstructive pulmonary disease (COPD), and his left arm was amputated above the elbow. His flute had 6 holes which is standard. Fortunately, the flute was 10 inches long and made of lightweight bamboo.

When I arrived, I asked Steve to hold the flute in his right hand to see what holes he could cover easily and naturally.

Steve's wife had a roll of duct tape.

I covered five holes on the flute to seal them off. Then, I instructed Steve on how to exhale in short forceful breaths to accommodate his COPD. I played an improvised melody on my flute and taught him how to add accent tones with his. Finally, I showed him how to play solos by creating one- and two-note songs on his small flute.

A week later, I saw Steve's wife at the Casa memorial held for surviving family members. She was radiant. She thanked me for teaching Steve to play his flute. Of his last week of life, she said, "It was the happiest of his life."

CHURCH

There was evidence of celebration as I pulled up to the house—pastel-colored crepe paper streamers and limp balloons strewn about. Inside, there were more crepe paper streamers and abandoned baskets with plush toy rabbits and small, fluffy, yellow, stuffed chicks.

I was there to change dressings on the patient's lower legs. The case manager stressed the importance of not skipping a day. The patient often complained, and the daughter, who was her caregiver, reported her mother resisted the dressing changes. As a result, some dressing changes had been skipped on weekends, and the wounds were not healing as rapidly as expected.

The patient's daughter had called earlier to request the visit be canceled because it was Easter Sunday. She explained, "We're Mormon. The whole family will be here for breakfast,

Easter baskets, an egg hunt, and church. The house will be full. It's going to be a zoo. I don't want the nurse coming and adding to the chaos. Mom is complaining more than usual."

I listened, commiserating, explaining how the case manager was concerned that healing was being delayed because weekend dressing changes were being skipped. We agreed I would visit while most of the family was at church. The daughter would be the only one at home with her mother.

"Mom's not in a very good mood."

I knocked softly on the patient's door and entered with supplies for the dressing change.

The patient was lying on her back on the near edge of a queen-size bed. Her head turned away, she responded, "HUMPH," when I greeted her.

I pulled back the bedding to expose bandages from knees to ankles. Kneeling on the carpeted floor to have the best access to the leg wounds, my head on the same level as the patient.

When I was almost finished, she abruptly turned to face me and made her stern declaration, "You should be in church!"

It seemed such an odd thing to say. *Was it because it was Easter? Would she have said this on an ordinary Sunday?*

Without giving it much thought, still on my knees, I looked into her eyes and gently responded, "This is my church."

JANE

Judy said, "The patient's daughter is visiting from Denver. Can you pick her up and take her out?"

"Take her where?"

"I don't know. The aide, who is there to bathe the patient, called for help. The daughter is going stir-crazy. She doesn't know anyone here and doesn't have a car. Can you get her out of there?" Judy pleaded.

When I arrived at the patient's small, isolated bungalow on American Lake, I saw a heavyset, red-haired woman standing in the yard talking on a cell phone and smoking a cigarette. The door was open. I was surprised when the woman hung up the phone, dropped her cigarette, and followed me inside.

There, a middle-aged woman wearing a "Franciscan Hospice" apron welcomed me with a smile.

I said, "I'm a volunteer. Judy sent me, she said you needed help."

The aide nodded toward the comatose patient on the bed. "I'm just here to give her a bath and change the linen." She rolled her eyes toward the patient's daughter who was pacing back and forth in the small room, running her fingers through her curly red hair. She was talking nonstop on the phone.

"I'm going crazy. I need to get out of here. I'm from Denver. I don't have a car. I need a cigarette. I can't smoke in here." She looked at the aide. "How long will you be here? I have to get out of here."

Without waiting for the aide to respond, she looked at me and asked, "Can you take me someplace where I can smoke?" Her wild red hair reminded me of a circus clown wig.

I nodded.

The woman, who said her name was Jane, got into my car and immediately lit a cigarette, saying, "Do you mind if I smoke?"

"Yes, I do mind. Please open the window so the smoke goes outside."

Jane complied and put the cigarette out in the ashtray.

I drove to a small bar-café in Lakewood which allowed smoking. When I explained to the hostess that I was a hospice volunteer and the woman with me needed a break and a cigarette, we were immediately seated at the bar.

Jane lit a cigarette and said, "I'll have a mocha."

The waitress looked puzzled, "What's a mocha?"

Jane became frantic, "A mocha? Don't you know how to make a mocha? A mocha is a mocha, I don't know how to make one!" She puffed furiously on her cigarette and looked like she might start crying.

The waitress looked very apologetic and said, "I'm sorry we don't have any mocha."

I assured the waitress it was okay and said, "Please bring me a cup of black coffee, a cup of hot chocolate, and an empty cup."

The waitress repeated my order, "Coffee, cocoa, and a cup," and hurried off. She returned a few minutes later with the requested items.

Jane did not seem to notice my earlier exchange with the waitress and said, "This is NOT what I ordered. I ordered a mocha!"

I carefully poured half of the coffee and half of the chocolate drink into the empty cup and handed it to Jane. "And here is your mocha."

Jane looked surprised, eyes widened. "Yes, of course! Mocha

is coffee and chocolate–why didn't I think of that?" She sipped her mocha, chain-smoked, and talked nonstop for 45 minutes, the agreed-upon time to take a break from her mother.

When I dropped Jane off, she said, "Thanks so much for the good visit. I feel so much better."

I smiled. "You're welcome."

Except for ordering coffee and hot chocolate, I had not said one word during our time together. Jane needed an ear for her venting. All I needed to do was show up.

GEORGIA

The call from Georgia's caregiver, Marjorie, came in as I walked through the office door. "Georgia is having trouble breathing."

I was immediately on my way.

Halfway to Georgia's home, Marjorie called again to say Georgia had died. Marjorie met me in the driveway, and I followed her around to the back of the house.

Georgia was lying with her head elevated on an aluminum lounge chair. She was wearing a white T-shirt and a disposable diaper. It was already 85 degrees in the dry Arizona heat when I pronounced death at 9:10 a.m. Flies were gathering, so I covered Georgia's body with a sheet. We had to get her body inside.

There was no way Marjorie and I could move Georgia's body without help. I called the mortuary, hoping they could help move Georgia's body inside and transport her there after friends and loved ones had all paid their last respects. I was told that they were operating on a skeletal staff for the weekend. They would only come once when the body was ready to be removed.

My next thought was to call 9-1-1 for assistance. Over the years, I had developed relationships with the police department and paramedics. They often came to help me. When I was just about to place the call, I noticed the circular gravel path leading from the patio to six or eight large pots holding three-foot-tall plants.

I could not believe my eyes! They were well-established marijuana plants!

I asked Marjorie, "Are those plants what I think they are?" I had only seen a marijuana plant once when the local police brought one for "show-and-tell" in hospice training.

Marjorie was nonchalant. "Georgia used marijuana to control pain. She grew her own to cut out the middleman." Marijuana was illegal in Arizona at the time. While we panicked in the heat over Georgia's dead body, a half-dozen curious neighbors had gathered at the corner of the house. I randomly enlisted the help of three strong men on either side of the chair who were able to move the chair with Georgia's body inside the bedroom.

I crawled onto the hospital bed to guide and receive Georgia's body, which was now wrapped in a sling created out of a sheet. I barked instructions: "Turn on the AC as cold as possible! Somebody, get ice bags to keep the body cool!" I finally lit some candles to help scent the air.

The team RN case manager and chaplain both knew about Georgia's use of marijuana, so for them, there was nothing to report on Monday. However, Casa co-founder, Lynette, had no knowledge of this. As I began to tell her, she prudishly covered her ears with her hands, shouting, "Stop! Stop! I don't want to hear about it!"

Catherine's Complaints

Catherine reminded me of a beached whale. She complained about everything: bed railings, the food, the room temperature, and her children not visiting.

She lived in Room 1 at Kanmar Place. Her ample 300-pound frame filled the twin-sized hospital bed and threatened to drape over the sides. She complained the half-bed rails were confining which is what they were intended to be. Staff was concerned that if Catherine turned over without the railing, she would topple onto the floor.

One weekend, while Catherine napped, her daughter and two sons got into a discussion about her care that escalated into an argument. Kanmar staff called Casa co-founder, Lynette, to mediate, and Lynette called me with instructions to call the Medical Director, Dr. David.

As nearly as I could ascertain, the argument centered around medication, with one son believing Catherine's medication was fine, and the other insisting she was being over-medicated.

When I called Dr. David, he asked, "What's the problem?"

I recall blathering on, skirting the issue of the brothers' disagreement.

Agitated, Dr. David asked me again, "What's the problem?"

Again, I blathered on, diplomatically skirting the real issue.

Frustrated, Dr. David asked a third time, "RuthiE, what *is* the problem?"

I blurted out, "The problem is she has two sons who are both doctors!"

With a sigh of relief, Dr. David responded, "Well, why didn't you say so! Put one of them on!"

There were no more complaints about medications. However, Catherine continued to be unhappy with everything, including my playing flute.

Patti, the RN manager of Kanmar, came to me and said,

"Catherine wants you to stop playing flute. She says she doesn't want to hear it."

I was outside of Room 5 at the opposite end of the building from Catherine's room. I had played native flute twice a week at Kanmar since it opened two years ago. Catherine's complaint was the first I'd ever received.

Patti said, "I think the music takes her to a place she doesn't want to go."

Perhaps that was true. I marched down the hall, knocked softly, and entered Room 1.

Catherine was lying on her right side facing the door.

I said, "Catherine, Patti told me you don't want to hear flute music."

She nodded without speaking.

I continued, "I come twice a week to play. I will not come into your room. I will play inside the rooms of other patients with the doors closed, and I will play as softly as I can. But sound carries, and you might still hear it. I am sorry if that happens, but I will not stop playing flute for the other residents.

I never saw her again.

Six weeks later Catherine passed away. I was "blown away"

when her daughter asked me to play flute at the memorial service which she was planning.

She said, "Mom loved your flute playing. She talked about it all the time."

I had a prior commitment and felt relieved to decline the invitation. To this day, I am conflicted about not playing for her. Was it that my ego was bruised when I heard that Catherine didn't want to hear me play, or was it that I knew that my playing would have soothed her spirit, making her less disagreeable as she transitioned? Perhaps my playing for Catherine one last time might have brought solace to both of us.

FAYE

Faye moved to Ireland when she retired. She was diagnosed with terminal cancer and came back to Tucson less than three months later to die. I expected to have a long relationship with her. She lived independently and enjoyed going out to lunch with her children several times a week and to church on Fridays.

When I would visit her, she would rest on top of the bed covers, propped up with several pillows, and close her eyes while I played native flute. When the music stopped, she would keep her eyes closed for several minutes of silence, then describe where the music had taken her in vivid detail. Faye was eager to draw but was critical of her attempts to be artistic.

"I can't draw," and "Lord, I'm not doing a very good job with drawing animals."

What Faye didn't understand was that her skill was not the

point. Drawing, or any 'mark- making,' is one of the ways a participant can use expressive arts. Because Faye had the strength to hold crayons and sit up, I suggested drawing and offered her materials to draw.

The first picture Faye drew was of cliffs above the ocean. She imagined she was standing at the highest point. "Close to Heaven," she said. "I feel ready to jump off, but I have no idea what is waiting for me."

Her voice was animated as she made scribbles across the paper and described her imaginings. "There is a shepherd named Daniel, and he and his sheep are hiding in caves among the rocks. There are grass puffins in nests, the wind is blowing, and waves are crashing far below."

When asked, she said the name of her drawing was *Searching*.

A week later, Faye's drawing was as calm as the first one was turbulent. She described a lush valley with a stream running through the center. Faye said she saw herself resting under a tree and watched as bands of horses came to drink at the stream. She spent several minutes attempting to draw a horse "so it would look like a horse," while continuing to describe her imagined scene. "I'm an observer," she said, "not an active participant." With reverence, she touched the paper on which she had not made a mark. The paper was purely a catalyst for her imagination to be unleashed. She continued verbally describing what she imagined.

"There are many different bands of horses. They are taking turns coming to the stream to drink. They are all so peaceful, and everyone is getting along. I call it *How Peaceful is My Valley*," she said proudly.

Faye looked up and made direct eye contact. "I believe this is what Heaven must be like, not so much how it looks, but the feeling of peaceful energy. It is like the bands of horses are my family, waiting to welcome me into Heaven."

I was devastated to learn that Faye died before our next scheduled session. I was grateful that I had said goodbye to her as though I may not see her again. I thanked her for allowing me to play flute for her and bring the arts in which she so willingly participated. It was clear that the arts helped move her from a state of anxiety about death to one of peace and acceptance.

NOT GOING TO LIVE LIKE THIS

There are many anecdotes of a patient living longer than anticipated in order to be present for an important event, such as the arrival of a loved one, a wedding, birth, or graduation. It also seems reasonable that a patient can choose NOT to continue living, if doing so would burden others or their own dignity. Refusing to eat or drink is a legitimate way a patient can hasten death, but could it happen overnight? I'll never know.

Elaine was a resident in Kanmar Place diagnosed with ALS (amyotrophic lateral sclerosis), a progressive neurodegenerative disease that affects the nerve cells in the brain and spinal cord. It is popularly called Lou Gehrig's disease. Elaine invited me into her room to thank me for visiting and playing flute for her. Her voice was calm and matter-of-fact as she said, "I couldn't lift my hands to the top of the tray table over the bed for lunch today. I decided a long time ago when someone had to feed me, I'm checking out."

Her bed was in an upright position. She demonstrated for me her inability to raise her hands above the tray table.

The next time I came to see her, her bed was empty. *I was just there.* Was it yesterday? A week ago? How did she die so suddenly? Did she have a stash of narcotics under her pillow that we didn't know about? No, she would not have been able to get them into her mouth. Elaine was the first person I ever met to tell me she would not live with limitations and died because of them.

My second experience with this phenomenon was Mr. Todd who moved from a SNF to live at home with his son. I do not recall why he was on hospice. It was common practice in our company for a nurse to visit whenever a patient transferred from a facility to home, or from home to a facility. The purpose for the visit was to see that the patient arrived safely and to help them settle in. We were also there to see if anything was needed like supplies, equipment, or medications.

Mr. Todd was a tall, slim man over six feet tall. He was perched on the edge of his new bed which was raised off the floor. His feet barely touched the floor. He was wearing a white undershirt and disposable diaper. His son, John, was in the next room working on the computer. Mr. Todd briefly introduced me when I arrived. John was 5'8" and told me he had a bad back. The special bed for his father would enable him to provide care without bending over.

Having finished my assessment, as I turned to leave, Mr. Todd called out, "John, I need to go to the bathroom."

John called to him, "Just go in the diaper, Dad. I will clean you up shortly."

Mr. Todd looked at me with sad eyes. "I won't live like this," he said.

I offered to help Mr. Todd to the toilet, but he declined. I still feel sad remembering this.

As a nurse, I understood John's logic. Given his back disability, a high bed and diapers would help him care for his father. However, it was a solution with which his father disagreed.

Mr. Todd died during the night. I would not have predicted this. He had been sitting on the side of his bed, clearly voicing his needs. I wondered again, how did this happen? Does the human mind just decide to die and the Spirit leaves on demand?

After a third patient died unexpectedly in what was clearly a choice not to be a burden on family, I have decided dying *can* be a choice. I was sent to check on Abuela (Spanish for grandmother). She had fallen and could not bear weight on her right leg. Abuela's family of three adult daughters, one with two teenaged sons, were from Mexico, and they had all purchased the house together.

When Abuela was diagnosed with cancer, they put her on hospice and brought her to live with them. She was 96 years old and did not speak English. Abuela's daughters asked questions of me.

"Does Abuela need to go to the emergency room?"

"Does she need an X-ray?"

I suspected her leg was broken. Remembering the hospice motto, *do the best you can with what you have*, I had the boys settle their grandmother onto a firm dining room chair, hoist her shoulder-high, then carry the chair between them to her bedroom.

I walked alongside her to make sure she was balanced and safe. Once tucked in and propped up with pillows and fully medicated for pain, I gathered the family in the living room and told them, "She must not be left alone."

The family huddled, like a coach planning a winning strategy with his team. Overhearing the conversation, it was clear one woman was in charge, creating a plan to rotate who stayed home. They all had entry-level, minimum-pay jobs: gas station attendant, hotel housekeeper, and fast-food cook. They were working out a plan on how they could get by, taking turns calling in sick.

I called Lisa, Casa's bilingual social worker on call for the weekend. I explained the situation and my concern. I wanted to make sure Abuela understood she must not get out of bed; she would be kept comfortable, and someone would be with her. Lisa was not sure she could come before she went off duty; however, she would see Abuela first thing in the morning. I begged her to make the visit today.

I needed to know that Abuela understood what was happening and that she was-reassured.

Lisa and I were stunned the next morning when informed that Abuela died during the night. Lisa was so glad I had insisted she visit.

Lisa said, "We had a wonderful chat. She was doing fine and

was grateful I came. She also said that she had been happy living with her daughters and grandsons. She also wanted me to know that she was fully independent until she fell." The last thing Abuela said was, "I do not wish to be a burden on my family."

Lisa and I agreed that her death was her decision.

PART 4
THE END

And, in Conclusion...

I have worked in hospice for over 30 years, yet death still remains the ultimate mystery. In my extensive training over the years, I have been taught the most simple ideas about death as well as more complex ideas such as "I am Spirit" and energy. I believe that in my efforts to unravel a straight path to understanding death, reflecting on life-after-life meditation is an opportunity to share what *I* imagine death might be like. Please join me in the experience.

I am lying on my back, eyes lightly closed, my head, neck, and spine are fully supported and comfortable. It feels like floating in a warm pool of water.

I take several deep, cleansing breaths, then inhale fully, sending the warm energy of my breath to sore, tight places in my body. As I exhale fully, discomforts in my body and mind are released.

With each inhale and exhale, my breath loosens and softens tight places. Gathered tension is exhaled. I feel more and more safe, more and more comfortable. The essence of Spirit of which I am part is inhaled, "Blessed am I, Spirit am I." Worry, fear, and all pain are dissolved and exhaled. Spirit's presence soaks into my skin, permeating each cell of muscle, tissue, and bone. I am resting on a cushion of energy.

I feel quiet inside and still, like a lake without ripples. The energy cushion supports and surrounds me, moving me gently forward. It draws in all the love and sweetness that has ever been felt for me by anyone at any time. I feel all the loving kindness that has ever been sent my way. Every prayer, good wish, every smile, and gesture of thanks, permeates and fills the field of energy around me. All the good I have ever given anyone comes back to me tenfold. My heart feels full of gratefulness.

Looking around, I recognize this place of safety

and comfort. I have been here before in guided meditations. It is the "safe place" I have always imagined Heaven to be. The air is warm with a soft, gentle breeze. Lush plants of many shades of green. The blue sky is streaked with pinks and reds of sunrise, oranges and yellows of sunset; shifting and changing. I hear music, soft and distant, familiar yet unrecognizable. The music changes tempo and volume riding on the colors; it swells and recedes in my heart like an incoming tide. Tears fill my eyes with the beauty of sound. A soft scent in the air reminds me of my mother's face powder. I feel the safe touch, being held on my father's lap, rocked in a rocking chair. A gentle touch of a hand on my shoulder. I recognize my maternal grandmother and others. I remember the wise and kind souls from my past who loved, supported, and guided me. My Guardian Angel, sweet spirits. Magical beings surround me. I feel their protection and support. We're moving forward, a casual rag tag marching band, holding hands so no one is left behind. There is expectancy and excitement. I know with certainty it is good and right for me to be here; this is where I need to be at this time. Something wonderful is about to happen.

Raising my eyes, I see a remarkable shining being–very far away–it is hard to distinguish at first, becoming discernable as it comes toward me. It emanates a full, soft aura of radiant light intensifying everything it shines on. I understand the pure essence of it all. Divine Spirit is with me. "I am the infinite within my soul." The intensity of love and wisdom is palpable as it approaches. Realization envelopes me. "WE ARE ALL ONE!"

I am released, freed from the divisions of life. Somehow, I am becoming part of this Unity. Somehow, I am being guided in some sort of second birthing–I am not dying–I am reaching the afterlife. The light comes up to me, bathing me in soft brightness–I feel the light as it touches my skin softly. I relax and let the light soak into me deeper and deeper. It permeates my body–compassionate eyes look at me. I feel the deep, kind gaze look into my eyes.

The bright light moves through me like a warm wave; I understand I am truly being seen, in all my complexity—in all my simplicity. I am seen, understood, acknowledged. As the light opens my heart softly and easily, it touches an ancient memory of who I really am, who I have always been and always will be. As I open to this sweet connection, enveloped in soft light—melting, merging, and molding into it—all of my pains, worries, and doubts disappear.

The loving gaze of this beautiful light being holds me with deep understanding. I have a sense of utter safety as I take in fully and deeply the love so freely offered. I feel my own love in return—free ... boundless—with understanding of the powerful circuitry between us, It is the same love that fills us both—the giver is the receiver; the receiver is the source.

The beauty of my life journey is seen with comprehension from the vantage of this powerful, healing light. Seeing it all—the pain, fear, hardship, all the courage, kindness, and love; the special gifts and abilities, moments of triumph and great beauty, the moments of despair and lost perspective—all of it is seen through the softness of the exquisite light.

I feel a new kindness toward myself and others, a

new forgiveness of myself and others for disappointments–letting it go–letting it go for seeing the truth of who I really am, fulfilling my purpose completely and beautifully attuned to this light, in harmony with all things, feeling love and gratitude for this awareness.

I know in the ground of my being, I can heal with the energy of my soul's loving kindness. That whatever seemed to be lost to me in this life still abides within me. That whatever I felt to be shattered by grief during life is still whole here. That whatever I thought unforgiving has already been redeemed here. Breathing in the power of this awareness and breathing out my gratitude, still aware of all the loving energy around me. I know it is mine eternally. I am aware of my special place in the Universe. The colors around me become brighter, the melodies sound more vivid, the air more intense.

I allow myself to rest here, safe in the just between. My breath slows, sensations of my body dwindle, like a candle flickering in the wind. Whenever it is time, just as smoothly and seamlessly as when the being of energy came to me, gently and easily moving on, it takes me with it, going back to wherever it came from. I feel a slight nip of energy separating from my heart center, leaving behind a physicality I no longer need.

I become part of the halo of this powerful loving light now encompassing what was once me. As I pass on with new awareness beyond life, after life, I hear my voice clearly state, "I give thanks for all that has been. I give thanks for all that is. I give thanks for all that is to come."

I breathe it in.

AHO (Amen)

ACKNOWLEDGMENTS

The door to hospice work was opened by Judy Green, my first supervisor. Stories from that world eventually became the foundation of this book. Writing stopped when forgotten anger surfaced. I thank Dr. Larry Lincoln for the reminder, "The only way out of the pain is through the pain."

The Buddhist proverb, "When the pupil is ready, the teacher will appear," became a reality with writing coach, Kim Green. This book took form from start to finish with Kim's superb coaching and guidance. I am deeply grateful.

"Tres amigas" held me accountable to complete Kim's assignments in a timely fashion: Francie Abbey, my Irish twin sister who has a discerning eye for perspective; Susie McCauley, my friend from "The Hawai'i Times" (1979) with whom we shared years of common interests, including writing;

and my beloved daughter, Anne Katherine Neilan Davis, an integral part of the book's beginning, middle, and end.

To Dr. Evan Kligman for "Life After Life" and permission to adapt it for my guided imagery of dying. Thank you.

Writing is part and parcel of my DNA. I acknowledge and celebrate all those who share it.